Know Thyself:
Nothing to Excess.
~Apollo's maxims to Delphi

Wings of Flame, Coils of Light:
A Devotional for Apollo

Edited and Compiled by Rev. Jonathan Sousa,
With especial thanks to those devotees and Priest/esses
who contributed to this Work of Vision.

Dedications and Thanks

Citing ancient tradition, I make a triple dedication of this work:

First, to the God Apollo. Without Apollo, my personal wounds would have festered in lieu of becoming doorways to grace and healing. For that, I offer Him love, adoration, and gratitude. I hope that this anthology pleases Him and assists those called by Him to walk more deeply with Him.

Second, to my Family of Blood and of Spirit, especially my mother Ann, my grandmother Rita, my nieces Rebecca and Lauren, my nephew Zachary, my coven family and extended lineage of the Craft, and those who have mentored me in both Craft and Art. Of these, great love and eternal thanks to Lori Bruno for guiding me to stillness and emerging as a mother to my spirit; to V.R and Scarlet of Rosa d'Oro; to B.M. of the Society of Diana (Fili d'Oro); and to those Mighty Ones who abide eternally in Elysium. I am so grateful for your teachings, your encouragement, and your compassion.

Third, I dedicate this to all who have contributed to its making. Thank you all, each of you, for sharing in this service to and for the Golden God.

Sincerely Yours,
Rev. Jonathan Sousa
Spring 2016

For you, Apollo!

Introduction

To say that this book is about and for Apollo seems a simple fact. And I truly hope that this offering finds favor with the Golden God. However, with all Deities, the only simply truth is that They are Mysteries. Beyond that, when we start pigeon holing Them or Their Works into comfortable categories for our ease… the Gods become limited in how they can affect us, work through us, and work with us.

Most will say that Apollo is a Greek God, adopted wholesale into the Roman pantheon. This is true, after a fashion, though His roots lie farther east.

Apollo is the Son of Leto and Zeus, born on the virgin isle of Delos. His twin sister is Artemis (Diana). However, in another legend, Leto gave birth to Her Twins whilst crossing the Tigris-Euphrates rivers. In Her labor, She clutched the riverbank. From the indentations of Her fingers, the first people arose to worship Her.

In Anatolia, Apollo's roots lie in the figures of Apulunas, Aipolos, and Adonis. Apulunus was a Wolf-Deity presiding over the practices of dream incubation, prophecy, and healing. Aipolos, meaning "the Goatherd", presided over the turning of the cosmic poles. In some fragments of legend and lore, Aipolos died by hanging upon a world-tree so that the poles would turn and the balance of nature be kept. The Roman Neoplatonists later identified Aipolos with Faunus and/or Pan. Lastly, Adonis – while evolving into a separate Deity amongst the Phoenicians and Greeks – was applied to both Apollo and Dionysos in Magna Graecia. Adonis, from the Semitic Adon, means "Lord."

In Minoan Crete, Apollo was identified or fused with their native Gods Zagreus and Pawayo. Zagreus is the son of Mother Rhea, and presided over agricultural mysteries of death and rebirth. In some of the ruins, He is equated to the Sun and to the Grape-Vine (as a tree of life). Zagreus was also identified with Zeus and Dionysos by later Mycenean Greeks. Pawayo, however, is directly antecedent to Apollo's later epithet of Paean, meaning a song of praise. Pawayo dealt with disease, both in its cause and in healing thereof.

We must also acknowledge the Sumerian Erragal (Nergal). Erragal was the Midday Sun who nonetheless descended into the Underworld to win the hand of the Goddess Ereshkigal. In doing so, Erragal became King reigning at Her side. This is mirrored by myths in Sicily and the rest of Magna Graecia, where the young Apollo enters the Underworld and courts Persephone. In order to woo Her, He fulfills twelve labors, each linked to one of the twelve signs of the zodiac. If this reminds us of the labors of Herackles (Hercules), it should. Herackles is a Greek adaptation of Erragal. It is interesting that, in the first lectirneistum of Rome, the Goddess Diana was paired, not with Apollo, but with Hercules. Only later, when Magna Graecia fell and the world only remembered Athens, in the second lectirneistum, was Diana linked directly with Apollo.

All of these clues contribute to an idea of Apollo vastly at odds with what most people assume Him to be. These assumptions derive from the Athenian exegesis, which sought to define the entirety of the ancient Greek world. Amongst the myriad other city-states in Hellas, Apollo was a darker God than the Athenians allowed. To the Athenians, Apollo was logic, reason, and beauty; He was patron of music and civilization; He was kindly disposed and shunned the Underworld. To everyone else, especially amongst the preSocratics, Apollo was a sorcerous God intimately linked to the Underworld. His was the meeting place between logic and intuition. His was the silence that allowed the Gods to speak directly to the Soul.

The Pythagoreans taught that the Sun itself was forged from the Underworld's fire. Thoughout Magna Graecia, Apollo's priesthood presided over chthonic Mysteries, magical rites, and ecstatic prophecy through dreaming trance. Most of His temples were built near volcanoes, sulphorous springs, or other doorways to the realms below. These associations and features survived in the Greek Magical Papyri, as well as in Apollo's cult outside of mainland Greece and Rome's heartland. In many ways, they still survive amongst practitioners of surviving Old Religions in Southern Italy.

Apollo was adopted directly from the Greeks by Rome. (Granted, Apollo's original Greek spelling was Apollon). He was especially revered as Apollo Medicus in His role as the healer of plague and excorcist of evil spirits. Rome identified Apollo, in its Imperial era, with many other Deities: Ianus Pater, Mithra, Sabazius, Soranus, Serapis, Harpocrates, Lugios, Maponos, Boraumus, Belinos, to name a few. The Emperor Augustus Caesar was particularly dedicated to Him.

During the Middle Ages, the Church alternated between seeing Him as a prototype of their Christ or as their God's alter ego, Lucifer. Both associations colored the survivals and revivals of Paganism and Witchery in both Italy and Greece.

And, in this modern era, the God is making Himself known: Patron of the Arts, God of the Sun and the Light Beyond the Sun, the Divine Physician, the Word of His Father, the protector of male homosexuals, athletes, artists, musicians, and healers, the friend of humanity who reminds us of our inate beauty and worth, the Lord of Sorcerers and Seers, and in so many more ways.

This book is an offering to, for, and about Apollo. It is my hope that this manuscript inspires, heals, helps, enlightens, challenges, and encourages the reader in relation to Him.

Apollo's Mythos: A Sampling of His Lore

The following are a synopsis of Apollo's exploits, trials, and accomplishments. They may be read as such for entertainment, for intellectual stimulation, and for devotional contemplation. Through the latter, these legends will be revived as *Mythos* – a Greek word that can be translated as a Mystery concerning the Gods, Their mutual relationship with humanity, and Their Wisdom (with how such Wisdom may benefit us, here and always).

This collection is drawn from primarily Greek and Southern Italian sources. The re-tellings are my own. Reading and sharing other variations (ancient and modern) can only enrich the experience. And, if the Muses favor you, the God may well unveil deeper variations particular to your own needs and the needs of those whom you choose to share such with.

Apollon Musegetes, lead the Nine Daughters of Memory from Mount Parnassus to assist me in the crafting that follows.

The Birth(s) of Apollo

All epiphanies of Apollo stress His close relationship with both His mother Leto (Latona) and His sister Artemis (Diana). Leto is the daughter Hyperion and Perses, ruling the night sky studded with Stars. Her sister, Asteria, is the mother of the Goddess Hekate. Artemis, Apollo's twin sister, shares many of Apollo's attributes, though has emerged as a lunar deity par excellence in modern Reconstructionist and Wiccan cultus. She, much like Her Itallic counterpart Diana, was and is much more than a chaste huntress.

The oldest versions of Apollo's cult come from ancient Anatolia, a region encompassing our modern Greece, Turkey, Libya, and parts of Russia. Here, Leto – heavy with child – crossed the Tigris-Euphrates rivers. During that voyage, she began to go into labor. As she came to the other bank, She clutched the shore and gave birth to two divine wolves: Artemis and Apollo. These two wolves attended Leto and followed Her wherever She went. (In some versions, Artemis and Apollo gained a more human visage after they were born.)

In these variants, there is no real mention of paternity. Commentators both ancient and modern have assumed – comparing them with Homer and Hesiod – that the father of both Twins was/is Zeus. This may be, or Leto may have given birth in an act of parthenogenesis.

On the Greek mainland, as enshrined by the poets and philosophers, the God Zeus came to Leto disguised as a bird. She conceived the Twins. As a result, Zeus' wife Hera cursed Leto so that She could never give birth on established land. Leto wandered, and – as each land turned Her aside – She grew fearful as Her belly swelled of where to claim sanctuary.

Zeus, pitying Leto and His unborn children, called upon His mother Rhea. Rhea, as an Earth Mother, caused two islands (Ortygia and Delos) to rise just as Leto came to them. On Ortygia, Leto gave birth to Artemis. On Delos, assisted by Artemis as a divine midwife, Leto gave birth to Apollo.

Artemis and Apollo were close, both to each other and to their mother. Queen Niobe boasted that Zeus had gifted her with seven daughters and seven sons, while Leto had only born one of each. Artemis slew the seven daughters of Niobe with her arrows of painless death. Apollo fired upon Niobe's sons with his venomous arrows of plague and pestilence.

In central and southern Italy, where Apollo and Diana were intimately associated with clandestine Mysteries and magical rites, Latona and Diana were identified (much as Demeter and the Kore were united). And so, ranging from Orphic tablets to the letters of Emperor Julian the ever-faithful to inscriptions from Beneventum in the Kingdom of Naples and early modern Tuscany (as collected by Charles Leland), we find the following sequence:

Diana, the Great Mother of Primordial Darkness, grew lonely. Reaching into Her Self, She divided Herself into light and shadow. The shadow (and the Moon) remained Diana. The light, embodied in the Sun, was Apollo. And, seeing that Apollo was so beautiful, Diana desired Him. Initially, Apollo balked and fled (setting the cycles of night and day into their sequence). However, when Diana prevailed and they consummated Their love, Diana Herself conceived and (in time) gave birth to all-holy Nature.

In other variants, especially popular amongst the Orphic and Neopythagorean schools, we find that Night (identified with Leto) gave birth to Phanes (the Primordial Light and Fire). Phanes was recognized as Apollo as cosmocrator (world-ruler). This birth took place in a cavern serving as a gate to the Underworld, where Night made Her home. Taking some of Phanes' Light and Fire, Night formed the Sun and set the Sun as Leader of the Stellar Gods and Guide Upon The Way of Return.

The Coming of Apollo to the Underworld (Southern Italian and Sicilian)

Apollo, the Divine Kouros (or Youth), descended across the River Styx into the Underworld. There, kneeling before the Queen, He asked Her to be His wife. The Goddess of the Underworld challenged Him to prove His worth first.

In some variants, She set Him four ordeals, possibly linked to the four elements espoused by Empedocles of Arigentum (whose followers told this story). In others, Proserpina sets the Kouros a series of seven (for the planets) or twelve (for the zodiac) labors.

In any case, the God is successful and returns before Proserpina's throne. She gives Him a scourge and a golden sword. The first gift shows that He is both the source of plague and the means of its cure. The latter shows Him as a champion of justice, which is one of the Underworld's most beloved daughters.

Apollo takes the name Pholarkos (Lord of the Lair) as Proserpina's mate. This aspect is intimately linked with Pythagorean teachings, as well as the practices of dream incubation and trance prophecy.

The Coming of Apollo to Delphi (Greek)

The caverns of Delphi were renowned for their links to prophecy and trance. A young woman came upon a fissure in the rock, and – knocked down by the fumes – began to speak with the tongue of Da (or Gaea as the later tribes called the Earth Mother). The woman's female descendants became Da's priestesses and periodically dispensed Her wisdom. In time, Da passed the growing temple and oracular work to Her daughter, Themis, Goddess of Truth, Divine Order, and Justice.

Per some of the oldest fragments, Themis passed Delphi's keeping to Apollo as a birthday gift.

Later retellings draw upon the wanderings of Leto. Hera had sent a dragon (the pythoness Delphyne) after Leto who, having harassed Leto, retired to the cave-oracle of Da and/or Themis. Once He came of age, Apollo strode to Delphyne's lair and exacted revenge. He took the masculine title Delphinus in honor of the deed, and christened the oracular site Delphi.

Apollo shared Delphi with His brother Dionysos. Some told (and retell) this as the result of the two Gods fighting, and Dionysos being victorious. Others will say that Apollo and Dionysos were lovers, and Delphi was the site where they made love. Still others will say that Apollo leaves Delphi for Hyperborea (the Northern Lands) where He is most at home, and asks Dionysos to preside there in His place. Lastly, on a mystical level, some will say that Apollo and Dionysos are two-sides of the same coin, two faces of one Ineffable Mystery: the Lord who is Light and Life to All in All.

The Lovers of Apollo (Greek and Itallic)

Apollo, like many of the Shining Ones, took many lovers. We have touched on a few, including His bond with His sister Artemis (Diana). With Artemis (Diana) and Persephone (Proserpina), Apollo also held the favors of Hekate, Pan, Selene, Eros, Hermes, Dionysos, Herackles, and Aphrodite Herself. Not much survives of the stories. Only epithets, inscriptions, and images tied to specific temples and areas.

The nymph Daphne fled from Apollo when He courted Her. She cried Her father, a River-God, to save Her. Her father turned Her into the laurel tree. Apollo was distraught and, weaving boughs from the tree, decreed that the laurel would be His crown.

Apollo loved the youth Hyakinthos dearly. However, Zephyros (the West Wind) was jealous, and desired Hyakinthos himself. When the latter resisted, Zephyros' desire turned to loathing. When Apollo and Hyakinthos were playing the discus, Zephyros blew the game-piece into a fatal shot. Apollo could not save Hyakinthos though some insist that Zeus granted Hyakinthos a second-life on Olympos with Apollo. His blood became the hyacinth flower. And Apollo instituted memorial games each summer solstice in His honor.

Apollo witnessed the Berber Goddess Kura (Hellenized as Kyrene) wrestling a lion. He fell in love on sight. The feeling was mutual. Later Greek legends will insist that He gave Her the entire land of Libya as a dowry and She bore His sons as the royal house therein. However, Libya was and is Kura's Land and territory from the start.

Apollo had once offended Zeus who condemned Him to live a time under the illusion of mortality. Thence punished, Apollo found Himself in the Thessalian regions, where King Admetus took Him on as shepherd and romantic companion. They were inseparable and maintained their relationship even after Apollo returned to His godly duties. This lasted until King Admetus crossed into Hades, and Apollo swore an oath to protect Admetus' lineage through the centuries.

Apollo also slept with each of the Nine Muses, enkindling the fire of gnosis in each of the Arts. One of the Muses gave birth to Orpheus, whose song could move rocks and cause the trees to dance. Orpheus fell in love with Eurydike. On their wedding day, the hunter Aristeaus (himself a son of King Admetus in some reckonings) fell in lust with Eurydike. She fled from Him, preferring Orpheus.

In her haste, Eurydike stepped upon an adder and died from its bite. Orpheus followed Her to the

Underworld and moved Persephone to allow Eurydike's return to life. However, Persephone stipulated that Orpheus could not look upon Eurydike until they had crossed into the realm of the living. Sadly, Orpheus glanced back just before crossing the gate, and lost Eurydike's second life. In despair, He sobbed. Maenads came upon Him and, desiring Him, tried to seduce Him. He rejected them, and they tore Him apart. In death, Orpheus was united with His beloved Eurydike.

Another of Apollo's sons was Asklepios (Ascelepiaus), the Divine Physician. However, Asklepios grew full of hubris and, when he cheated Hades by reviving the Dead, Zeus killed Him with a thunderbolt. In retaliation of this, Apollo killed one of Zeus' favorites. In some reckonings, this is the crime for which Zeus punished Apollo to live as a shepherd.

On a more personal level, Apollo was known for taking His priestesses and priests as lovers in sacred marriage. (Certain of His priesthood shared a title with some of Dionysos' priesthood i.e. they were known as the 'Brides of the God'.) In Southern Italian Craft traditions, this is recognized as the root for what the meideval church called the incubus or demon lover. However, that association may or may not be historically accurate.

The Musical Battle (Greek)

The shepherd Marsyas boasted that he was the best musician in the world. Apollo challenged Marsyas to a musical duel. In some versions, the Goddess Athena was the judge. In others, the Nine Muses fulfilled this role. In either case, Apollo won the competition. Maryas grew the ears of a jackass. Yet, he still continued to insist that he was better than Apollo. The Furies rose and skinned Marsyas for his hubris. (In some versions, Apollo flayed him Himself).

The Epiphany of the Muses (Greek and Italian Renaissance)

Mnemosyne, Goddess of Memory, lay with Zeus, and gave birth to the Nine Muses. The Muses were and are the Goddesses of the Arts, Sciences, and the Heroic Ideal. They gravitated to Apollo who leads their chorus on the slopes of Mount Parnassus. Their song is known colloquially as the Harmony of the Spheres. Legend dictates that, when they stop their Song, then all creation itself will cease to be.

The Nine Muses are:

Calliope, ruling Epic Poetry.
Clio, ruling History.
Euterpe, ruling Music, Song, and Elegiac Poetry (i.e. the eulogy).
Erato, ruling Lyric Poetry and Erotic Pleasures.
Melpomene, ruling Tragedy.
Polyhymnia, ruling Hymns and Agriculture.
Thalia, ruling Comedy.
Ourania, ruling Astronomy (and its sister Astrology).

Correspondences

The following correspondences are drawn from historical practices and traditional lore. They are by no means exhaustive, but are offered as starting points for contemplation, further research, and personal piety.

Divine Syncretisms

Much of the following derives from antiquity, as Apollo's cult interfaced with other religions and cultures. The same could be said for His continuing (albeit subversive) worship in modern Greece, Armenia, and Italy. Lastly, a portion derive from the likes of Crowley's 777 and other modern methods of correlation (often deriving from the Golden Dawn's synthesis of religion and magic).

With regards to archaic syncretism, opinions differ as to whether such assert that Deity A equals Deity B, if it were a means of explaining Deity A to worshippers of Deity B by means of comparison, or if there was an acknowledgement that Deity A and Deity B were unified in expressing the same Power, albeit in ways that were particular to a given time or culture. At times, any one of these theories could hold true. And, at other times, all these theories (and more) could also have been true.

Graeco-Italian: Aplu, Apollo, Attys, Dionysos, Herackles, Trophonios, Orpheus, Asklepios, Hermes, Iaakhos, Kouros, Hyakinthos, Zeus, Pan, Faunus, Zagreus, Lupercus, Typhon, Sol Invictus, Lucifer, and Serapis

Middle Eastern: Adonis, Elegebal, Mithra, Reshep, Nergal (Erragal), Heru-Ur, Heru-per-khraad, Sutekh (Seth), Baal Shemain, Baal Karnayin, Ra-Heruakhty, Wesir, Melquart, Hubal, Apulunas, Enki (Ea), Melek Taus, Shamash (Uttu), and Ashur.

Northern European: Baldur, Loki, Freyr, the Bucca, Belenus, Grannus, Vindonos, Moggens, Lugios, Lugh Lamfhada, Mabon ap Modron, Maponos, Arawn, Gwynn ap Nudd, Oghma, Ogmios, Pwca, Teutates, Esus, and Veles (Volos)

Judaeo-Christian (orthodox and heretical): The Cosmic Christ (the Logos of the Father), Lucifer / the Devil, Apollyon/Abbadon, Saint Michael the Archangel, Saint Lucy, Saint Anthony of Padua, Saint Francis of Assissi, Saint Nicholas, Saint Luciferus of Sardinia, Metatron, Enoch, Elisha, Tubal Cain, Azazel, Lumiel, Saint John the Baptist, the Christ Child, and the Crucified Jesus.

Divine Allies

The following are Deities who have traditionally shared sacred space amicably with Apollo in His varying aspects. As a Deity of colonization, Apollo's light touched (and was touched by) many cultures and creeds.

Graeco-Italian: Agathos Daimon, Aradia, Artemis, Diana, Leto (Latona), Alexander the Great, Hyakinthos, Kyrene, Daphne, Orpheus, Asklepios (Asclepiaus), Aphrodite (Venus), Athena (Minerva), Hermes (Mercurius), Dionysos (Bacchus), Herackles (Hercules), Trophonios, Da (Gaea), Rhea, Mnemoysyne, the Nine Muses, Medea, Hekate, Kirke, Zeus, Fufluns, Teramo, Pan, Faunus, Hera (Iuno), Persephone (Proserpina), Nyx, Eurynome, Ophion, Augustus Caesar, Nero, Julian the Ever

Faithful (called the Apostate by some), Fortuna, and Demeter (Ceres). Also, may be venerated with the Pythia of Delphi and/or the Sybil of Cumae.

<u>Middle Eastern</u>: Athirat of the Sea, Astarte, Anath, Mithra, Sol Invictus, Inanna, Ereshkigal, Naamah, Herodias, Auset, Hwt-Hrw, Nebet-Hwt, Arsinoe III, Cleopatra, Elegebal, Cybele, Atargatis (Derceto), Baal Karnayim, Baal Shemain, Shamash (Uttu), Heru, Sutekh, Hubal, Allat, Al-Uzza, Dushara, El Aswad, Iblis, Sakyamuni Buddha, and Mahavaircona Buddha.

<u>Northern European</u>: Freyja, Freyr, Rosmerta, Damona, Brigindo, Brighid, Sirona, Sequana, Belenos, Vindonos, Lugios, Ogmios, Taranis, Teutates, Esus, Hu Gadarn, Elen of the Ways, Arawn, Mabon ap Modron, Arthur Pendragon, Morgana la Fey, Woden, Frau Holda, and Epona.

<u>Judaeo-Christian (orthodox and heretical)</u>: The Shekinah, the Sophia, the Holy Spirit, Our Lady of Mount Carmel, Our Lady of Lourdes, Saint Seraphim the Wonder Worker, Saint Artemidoros, Saint Eleutherios, Cain, Naamah, Tubal Cain, Herodias, Saint Anne, Saint Lucy, Saint Agatha, Saint Rosalie, Saint Michael the Archangel, Saint Raphael the Archangel, the holy guardian angels, Judas Iscariot, El Shaitan, Lucifer, Lumiel, Azazel, Jehovah, and Apollyon/Abbadon.

Festivals and Holy Days

In Greek tradition, the seventh day of each month belongs to Apollo. Traditionally, this would be the seventh day after the new moon. However, this may also apply to the seventh day of each solar month.

The Thargelia, which traditionally takes place seven days after the New Moon in late May or early June, celebrates the birthdays of both Apollo and Artemis. The Thargelia featured the excorcism of miasma (impurity) through use of a pharmakhos (or scape goat). It was and is also a celebration of the first fruits, and so was shared with both Demeter and Rhea in antiquity. In Roman times, the Thargelia was typically fixed to the end of May. This has led some modern devotees to keep the feast on Memorial Day weekend, incorporating a libation to our Fallen Heroes (and Heroines).

The Solstices were especially sacred to Apollo in Greek lore. At the Winter Solstice, Apollo left Delphi in the hands of Dionysos, and retreated to his "favored country" of Hyperborea. The Summer Solstice welcomed Apollo back to Delphi as Dionysos wandered the world. The Summer Solstice also marked the death (and possible resurrection) of the God's lover, Hyakinthos.

The Romans dedicated several feast days for Apollo.

The Lupercalia (February 13-15) was so old that the Romans were never sure exactly to whom it was sacred to. Apollo (as Lysius i.e. wolfish) received honors at several points in the history of Rome's Imperium at this feast. It featured a goat sacrifice and purification by young men wielding scourges.

The Liberalia (March 17th) was officially dedicated to Liber Pater (Bacchus) and Libera (Proserpina). However, under Augustus Caesar, Apollo was included in the portion when young men first donned the clothes of an adult.

July 13-16th were dedicated to Apollo in his medical and athletic aspects. Games, competitions, and races (foot and equestrian) were featured at this time. In some areas, there were also musical and/or bardic competitions.

A harvest festival on September 23rd was shared between Apollo and his mother Latona.

Incidentally, the poet Sallustius ascribed the sun sign Leo to Apollo's rulership.

In modern times, those coming from a modern / eclectic Neopagan background have focused devotion upon Apollo on the Quarter Days (Solstices and Equinoxes). Some will also acknowledge Him at Beltaine (May Day) due to His links to Belenus. This is because the Phoaceans (a Greek tribe famed for exploration) identified Hyperborea with the British Isles and the Baltic Sea region.

Herbs and Plants

Bay laurel, frankincense, amber resin, yellow sandalwood, holy basil, lightning-touched oak, apples, pears, peaches, St John's Wort, cinnamon, ginger, henbane, patchouli, ivy, grapevine, wormwood, mugwort, barley, wheat, carrots, heliotrope, sunflower, morning glory, cypress, mullein, foxglove, olives, garlic, onions, lemons, oranges, mangoes, spearmint, lavender, rowanberries, hazel, almonds, and (per group gnosis from American devotees) maize or corn.

Minerals

Gold, pyrite, platinum, silver, pyrite, citrine, garnet, amber, white or clear quartz, peacock ore, serpentine, basalt, salt, yellow ochre, red ochre, and aquamarine.

Animals (Common and Mythical)

Dolphins, whales, serpents, dragons, griffins, the nautilus, unicorns, stags (especially white stags), wolves, dogs, hawks, falcons, goats, bulls, rams, lions, hyenas, robin redbreast, peacock, ravens, crows, turkey vultures, mockingbirds, tigers, domestic cats, centaurs, horses, and monkeys.

Colors

For his solar aspects, gold, yellow, and orange. Also, light blue and royal violet.

For his chthonic aspects, scarlet and deep red, with indigo and saffron shades.

In general, white, yellow, and blue.

Numbers

The number 7 is intimately associated with him. That said, following Pythagoroas, he can be identified with any and all numerals as the Idea of Numeration that produces the Forms of individuated life. His followers ascribed the Tetraktys as an ikon of the God, which encompassed the numbers One through Ten in Four rows.

In the Hermetic Quabbalah, Apollo is linked to 6 (the sphere of Tiphareth as Solar King and Divine Child), to 9 (the sphere of Yesod in his role as psychompompos and progenitor), to 8 (the sphere of Hod as Magos, Healer, and Prophet), to 2 (the sphere of Chockmah, because of his twinship with Artemis), and 1 (the sphere of Kether as Primordial Unity).

Libations & Offerings

In general, Apollo appreciates offerings of spelt grain, barley, wheat, bread, wine, meade, and donations in support of either the causes or those creatures that he loves (including artists, musicians, GLBTQ, and medical research). If you are a musician or artist, offerings of your work earn his favor. If not, learning an art or musical instrument is a worthy dedication for your devotion. Also, flowers and fresh fruits.

In his more popular associations (solar, music, healing, prophecy, etc), he is intimately drawn to frankincense and bay laurel. Images of his sacred animals are also traditional. Per current gnosis amongst Hellenic and Roman Reconstructionists in the USA, he has also developed a fondness for Tex-Mex cooking!

In his less popular roles (the underworld, sorcery, ecstastic trance, cathartic healing, etc), he accepts offerings of one's blood (your own), effigies burnt in toto and their remains buried, sacred pledges (anciently known as the god-bargain or dedication i.e. an oath to do something significant in exchange for his aid), sleeping in a sacred space (especially if requesting his aid through dream oracles), austerities (especially fasting and scourging), dancing to ecstatic music, absinthe, and rum.

An Apollonian Playlist

Apollo is the Lord of Song and Leader of the Muses. As such, ALL forms and facets of music express His divinity, earn His favor, and celebrate His gifts to humanity. The following are some personal favorites (per the suggestions of Moondancer, Dana Corby, Gwendolyn Reece, Kyrene Araidne, Sarah Robla, Ma'at Hemlock, Rosaleen Penner, Beth Ann Mastromarino, and others).

Classical Artists: Bach, Beethoven, Mozart.

Artists In General: Daemonia Nymphe, Laboratorium Piesni, Blackmore's Knight, Loreena Mckennit, Allessandra Belloni, Prince, Jimi Hendrix, Shine Down, Godsmack, Vas.

Individual Selections:

Apollo: Atmosphere & Soundtrack (Brian Enos)
Auld Sang Lyne (Mothertongue adaptation)
Beautiful Boy (Inkkubus Sukkubus)
Burn Fire (Mothertongue)
Burning Bright (Shine Down)
Circle of Life (Elton John)
Dante's Prayer (Loreena Mckennit)
Defying Gravity (Idina Menzel)
Different Colors (Walk the Moon)
Dig (Incubus)
Evolve (Gaia Consort)
Firebird's Child (SJ Tucker)
Fundamentum (Lesiem)
Hanging by a Moment (Lifehouse)
He Lives in You (Lebo M et al)
Horns of the Goat (Inkkubus Sukkubus)
Hymn to Herne (SJ Tucker)

I Dare You (Shine Down)
Kyrie (Mister Mister)
Let It Go (Idina Menzel)
Lightning Crashes (Live)
Loved By The Sun (Tangerine Dreams)
Lucifer (Inkkubus Sukkubus)
The Mill of Magick (Gypsy)
Mystic's Dream (Loreena Mckennit)
Neptune (SJ Tucker)
Nothing Else Matters (Metallica)
Oh Hey (Lumineers)
One Word(POD)
Ophelia (Lumineers)
Renegades (X Ambassadors)
Return to Innocence (Enigma)
Saint Cecilia (Fu Fighters)
Saltatio Vita (Omnia)
Serenity (Godsmack)
Shut Up And Dance (Walk the Moon)
Sol Invictus (Thea Gilmore)
Something More (Switchfoot)
Sound of Silence (Simon & Garfunkel)
The Sun God (Gwydion Penderrwen)
Sunyata (Vas)
Sztoj Pa Moru (Laboratorium Piesni)
Undefeated Sun (Steeleye Span)
Voodoo (Godsmack)
We Want a World (Gypsy)
Witchdoctor (DeStat)

Resources for Further Research

Websites

http://apollospythia.com/pythagoreanism/daily-pythagorean-practice/

http://web.eecs.utk.edu/~mclennan/OM/index.html

http://www.hellenion.org

http://www.juliansociety.org

http://www.magika.org

http://www.mysteriousetruscans.com/religion.html

http://www.novaroma.org

https://www.peterkingsley.org

http://www.sacred-texts.com/

https://www.facebook.com/TheSocietyOfDiana

http://societyofdiana.blogspot.com

http://stregacrafts.com

ww.TempleApollo.com

http://www.theoi.com

http://trinacrianrose.weebly.com

https://web.eecs.utk.edu/~mclennan/BA

http://thewitchesalmanac.com/

Books

Adkins & Adkins. Handbook to Life in Ancient Rome.
Agrippa, Cornelius. Three Books of Occult Philosophy.
Bernstein, Frances. Classical Living: Reconnecting With the Rituals of Ancient Rome.
Betz, Hans. The Greek Magical Papyri In Translation.
Boer, Charles (translator). The Homeric Hymns.
Bonefry, Yves. Roman and European Mythologies.
Bowden, Hugh. Mystery Cults of the Ancient World.

Bradley, Marion Zimmer. The Firebrand.

Broad, William. The Oracle.

Buckley, Natalie. Paiawon Apollo The Sun God.

Burket, Walter. Greek Religion.

Connely, Joan Breton. Portrait of a Priestess.

Conner, Randy. Blossom of Bone: Reclaiming the Connections Between Homoeroticism and the Sacred.

De Biasi, Jean-Louis. Rediscover the Magic of the Gods and Goddesses.

DeMonte, Nicola. Secrets of the Orphic Gold Tablets.

Dunn, Patrick. The Practical Art of Divine Magic.

Edmunds, Radcliffe. The Orphic Gold Tablets and Greek Religion.

Elworthy, Thomas. The Evil Eye.

Evans, Arthur. Witchcraft and the Gay Counterculture.

Farrar, Janet & Stewart. The Witches' God.

Frazer, Sir James. The Golden Bough.

Gaffney, Mark. Gnostic Secrets of the Naasenes.

Gates, Doris. The Golden God.

Ginzburg, Carlo. Ecstasies.

Ginzburg, Carlo. The Night Battles.

Graf, Fritz. Apollo.

Graf, Fritz. Magic in the Ancient World.

Graves, Robert. The Greek Myths.

Guthrie, Kenneth & Fideler, David. The Pythagorean Sourcebook & Library.

Gwynn. A Light from the Shadows: A Mythos of Modern Traditional Witchcraft.

Hall, Manly P. The Secret Teachings of All Ages.

Howard, Michael. The Book of Fallen Angels.

Howard, Michael. Pillars of Tubal Cain.

Illes, Judika. Encyclopedia of Spirits.

Jackson, Nigel. Masks of Misrule.

Kerenyi, Carl. Apollo: The Wind, the Spirit, and the God.

Kerenyi, Carl. Gods of the Greeks.

Kingsley, Peter. Ancient Philosophy, Mysticism, and Magic.

Kingsley, Peter. In the Dark Places of Wisdom.

Kingsley, Peter. Reality.

Kupperman, Jeffrey. Living Theurgy.

Leland, Charles. Aradia or the Gospel of the Witches.

Leland, Charles. Etruscan Roman Remains.

Lindahl, Carl, et al. Medieval Folklore.

Martello, Leo. Black Magic, Satanism, & Voodoo.

Martello, Leo. Witchcraft: The Old Religion.

Meyers, Marvin. The Ancient Mysteries.

Mierzwicki, Tony. Graeco-Egyptian Magick.

Michelet, Jules. La Sorciere.

Mishev, Georgi. Thracian Magic.

Oates, Shani. Tubelo's Green Fire.

Opsopaus, John. The Pythagorean Tarot.

Ovid. The Metamorpheses.

Rahn, Otto. Lucifer's Court.

Ristic, Radomir. Balkan Traditional Witchcraft.

Scott, Michael. <u>Delphi.</u>

Sousa, Jonathan. <u>Classical Polytheism.</u>

Sousa, Jonathan et al. <u>Reflections in Diana's Mirror.</u>

Sousa, Jonathan. <u>Witchheart.</u>

Stagman, Myron. <u>100 Prophecies of the Delphic Oracle.</u>

Taunton, Gwendolyn. <u>Kratos: The Hellenic Tradition.</u>

Taylor, Thomas (translator). <u>Emperor Julian's Oration to the Sovereign Sun.</u>

Taylor, Thomas (translator). <u>The Orphic Hymns.</u>

Valiente, Doreen. <u>ABC of Witchcraft Past and Present.</u>

Versilius, Arthur. <u>Philosophy of Magic.</u>

The following offerings are shared by Priestesses and Priests,
Mystics and Magi,
Witches and other Rebirthers of the Ancient Ways,
all sharing in devotion to the far-Shining Lord, our beloved Apollo.

How Apollo's laurel sapling shakes!
How the whole temple shakes! Away, away with the wicked!
It must be Phoebus kicking at the door with his fair foot.
Do you not see? The Delian palm nods gently,
All of a sudden; the swan sings beautifully in the air.
Bolts of the doors, thrust yourselves back.
Keys--open the doors! For the god is no longer far away.
- Hymn to Apollo, Callimachus

My Life With Apollo Goes Beyond a Mere Title (Kyrene Ariadne)

There are many books out there about Apollo, some of the best ones being out of print such as Karl Kerenyi's *Apollo: The Wind, the Spirit, and the God*. Hymns from ancient times by Homer and Callimachus sing praises to him and name a number of his attributes. A person can read them all, memorize them all, and whether or not you buy Carl Jung's notion of Apollo as being of light, logic, and rationality, the truth is that no one can describe Apollo better than someone who honors him personally on a regular basis. And that is why I'm writing this for everyone who wants to know more about him, either out of curiosity, a deeper understanding as a Hellenic polytheist, or someone who just had a spiritual encounter with him and is dying to comprehend more of what they're in for in regards to the god in their lives.

When I first thought of submitting an essay on Apollo for this anthology, I thought perhaps of something more of a scholarly bent. But then I remembered all of the times I wanted to get to know a deity better and what I got the most out of when I went to go research, and the most useful information beyond scholarly texts always came directly from the mouths of worshippers, either ancient or well-researched modern ones. Here's the good news: we still exist today and there are plenty of us to tell the tale. The bad news is that Apollo is a very, very, very complicated deity and one writing piece alone is not going to cut it. All I can do is hope that whatever I manage to convey helps guide someone on their next steps of their introduction to the god, and try not to write an entire book in the process!

The best place to begin talking about Apollo is at the beginning: my beginning. At aged nineteen I was in college studying for my Bachelors in Computer Science. I had been a polytheist for the past five years and was regularly gathering for rituals with my local ADF Druidic group, actively involved in Irish polytheism with the Daghda, the Irish all-father, as my guide and main god, and partaking of Tibetan Buddhist meditations on the side. Everything was nice, neat, and tidy. I thought "patron deity" meant "deity you pray to frequently and has maybe manifested in a dream or two", as ignorant on the subject as a virgin is in regards to how sex is actually like. Then one morning that summer Apollo showed up in a very intense and vivid dream, and threw a wrench in the works. I had *no* idea what to do with this new god, who seemingly arrived out of left field, and wondered if it was merely a fluke. It was not.

As a result of the experience I dove into my college's library, and learned a ton about Apollo. Naturally it all made sense—too much sense. Writing, dreams, prophesy, music, art, even crows. It was all tying in perfectly with my life in uncanny ways I hadn't even thought of and weird events kept happening to me. I had dreams about variations of his name and details about the Delphic Oracle and its excavations which I later researched and found to be factual. Truth bombs just kept dropping and showed no signs of slowing down, and if I had wanted signs that the god was indeed very interested in being a major part of my life, they definitely came. The very last message I received from the Daghda about three days after it all started was "Apollo will require the most amount of responsibility."

The Daghda wasn't kidding. My research online inspired me to create the first emailing list for Hellenic polytheism called HellenicPagan on Onelist, which later became eGroups, and now is Yahoogroups. It also exists as a group on Facebook. From that list I gathered some people together and started Hellenion, an international Hellenic polytheistic organization. Lots of big wheels came turning after he came into my life, and I can't picture what my life would've been like if he hadn't. Since Apollo's arrival, I've dedicated myself to him in the community as a priestess of his and like a few others who are devoted to him in similar ways, wear an amber ring in honor of him on my left hand. I consider that ring to be a symbol of the sacred bond I have with him. It's very much a spiritual marriage in a lot of ways, something which is deeply personal to me and I rarely have talked about publicly. He means a lot to me and has made a huge impact on me and my interaction with the world, and as corny as it sounds, the god is my sunshine.

Apollo is indeed a god of sunlight, but he's also a god who is described by Homer in the Iliad as "descending upon the Greeks like the night", and that's not meant to be an ironic description. One of the things I've found is that he's a god with a lot of layers, is very intense, but is also very kind. He often comes to people who are healers, psychics, artists, athletes, and musicians. Like many gods, he not only deals with these forces but in their opposite—which in mastery of any subject should make a great deal of sense. To truly own any particular trade or accomplish anything, you need to master all of its aspects. If you know how to code software that works you'll also need to know how to make software that doesn't. If you get allergy shots, you're injected with a bit of what you're allergic to in order to build up your tolerance. Any medicine given in large enough dose becomes a poison, and that which can heal can also kill. Apollo Iatros, or Physician Apollo, also knows how to bring plague, and any creator would know how to destroy.

The primary aspect I've dealt with Apollo is in his role as the Pythian, Apollo Pythios: prophesy, psychic dreams, and divination. I've met Reiki practitioners who also honor Apollo as well. As a deity of purification and healing, one could also argue that he'd be an ideal deity for someone who is interested in essentially performing the Greek equivalent of exorcisms, consecration, or any sort of ritual cleansing. People who are writers or musicians would do best to honor him as well.

Cleansing is definitely Apollo's thing. He's a god who cleans house, and he's not going to beat around the bush about it. If there's anyone in your life who is a total leech on you and your resources, he will let you know under no uncertain terms that the offending person must go, and they will be cast out of your life whether it's desired or not. It won't always be a pleasant experience, but you'll be thankful later, trust me. Apollo will do this not just with people, but things. It could be jobs, homes, things— entire lifestyle changes. However if this happens to you, you *will* wind up in a far, far better place afterwards with zero regrets. That's a guarantee.

I'm forever thanking him for his presence in my life in ways both formal and informal. For offerings, I typically burn a blend of frankincense and bay. Sometimes a little cinnamon will be thrown in for good measure. Water or wine make for good libations as well, and I've found that cognac makes for a good offering and mead as well. I rarely offer food, but if you're doing a festival or ritual in his honor and want to eat after saving some of it for him is generally a good idea. Anything with bread, spicy food, olives and/or olive oil are all good things. He likes attention and as a god of truth and oaths, he appreciates sincerity far more than precision or perfection. Just pray and speak to him from the heart. Even if you're rambling nonsensically at his altar or shrine, regardless of whether or not you're doing a formal ritual just be yourself. That's all.

Interestingly I've found that a lot of Apollo's followers are inspired to go pescatarian, vegetarian, or even vegan—I myself wound up going vegan out of the blue and I frankly blame him! It's not a requirement but if your diet and/or lifestyle changes as a result of his impact on your life, don't be surprised. Anything which is good for the sake of ritual purity and/or your overall health and he'll be on it. It's generally a good idea to take good care of yourself anyhow as Apollo is a god of health and healing, so even if you decide to eliminate or cut back on animal products (or just wind up doing so because your body suddenly becomes intolerant to them like mine did) please don't become a junk food vegetarian or vegan and eat nothing but pasta and sugar! He won't like that either, trust me.

Not every person who is drawn to the god will necessarily be mystical in inclination, and even if they are, not everyone who is mystical in inclination will be drawn towards the mantic arts. I myself am both a mystic and a seer, and I've frequently done tarot and other forms of divination for others in honor of the god. A few caveats on the Pythian: he's intense. Really, really, really, really intense. But he means well. Every psychic dream I had turned into a nightmare before Apollo showed up in my life, and he helped me to calm and center myself so I wouldn't freak out every time it happened. I owe him a huge debt of gratitude for that alone. But he will be pushing the envelope and encouraging you to grow, develop, and evolve. I've found Apollo to be big on spiritual and personal evolution, and there is no such thing as doing too much personal development where he is concerned. I've never found Apollo to be excessive or a jerk about it however; he's always been in my experience to be exceedingly patient and caring. Just do your best, strive for *areté* (a lovely Greek word denoting virtue and excellence, especially moral excellence), and that's basically all you really need to do.

One thing which must be mentioned, especially from those who are more used to mainstream religions and faiths: honoring the gods isn't just something you do at your altar or in the occasional habitual prayer or ritual. It's about being mindful of their influence in your life and making your life into something which not only makes you a better person but also enables you to interact with the world better and bring what is important to them into the world. That something better could be writing, music, poetry, art, Reiki, medicine, tarot and other methods of divination, life coaching, counseling, athletics—anything which is essential to you and aligns with whatever gods you are honoring. I can't begin to emphasize how important this is, this holistic view of being a Hellenic polytheist and/or devotee of Apollo or any other deity. Whatever you are good at, enjoy, and calls to your heart, remember the gods who have that in their sphere and that alone is just as good as an offering. The act of doing such and the mindfulness of it *is* that offering.

No matter what you do in your worship of the god, just remember that in his tales Apollo is known for saying "Everything in moderation...including moderation." Balance in everything is key. This means balancing your physical, mental, emotional, and spiritual lives and making sure they're all healthy and in harmony. It'll be a constant upkeep, something you'll always be working on, and that's okay. The god knows you're human too.

I maintain an online temple to him at www.TempleApollo.com and run a Facebook page called the Delian Oracle at www.facebook.com/thedelianoracle. On my online temple I keep a list of resources and books about Apollo. If you ever want to reach me for any reason, whether you want to learn more about Apollo, Hellenic polytheism in general, want to submit something to the temple site, and/or are in need of an oracular reading I can be reached either at kyrene@delianoracle.com or kyrene@templeapollo.com.

le Paian

When I am still and I listen
I hear your song and it brings me peace
Like the warmth of the sun upon me
I feel you near
O golden haired archer, shining and radiant
I look up to that bright light through you
Beyond the ineffable
Lord of the song and of truth
I would sing for you gladly to have you near
There is a moment of silence and I pray
For the vision of the warmth of your smile
And your presense always
It beckons in my heart, this gladness
And I know that you with bow outstretched
Are watching over me
Peace fills me
You who gives me dreams and fills me with words beyond words
And songs beyond songs
All from that sparkling Source unimaginable
Shining Lord of Delphi
Oh Lord, oh Lord, oh Lord
Grant me the ability to see where my strength lies
So that I may have the courage to gaze up into your shining face
And spread the joy of your Light to all whom may see and hear
Of you, dear Phoebus
Lord of Light, oh Distant Archer
May you never be distant from me
And near always
For you have my heart and soul
And from the depths of my being
Pours praise and devotion to you, to the heavens above
For thanks that you are near me
That I may somehow touch the sky
And gaze upon it with wonder
As I do your shining face
I adore thee and I call upon thee always
For my heart and you are One,
Apollon.

~~ Kyrene

Here comes the Sun! (Ariel Manohara)

I was the first male ordained as a priest within *École des mystères de la Déesse* which has members in Francophone countries and centers most importantly on the Goddess. I quickly felt the need to explore and build a relationship with the Divine Masculine so I enrolled in their "Beloved God exploration" which is a self-guided course. Now, I had to find a specific god to get to know… Despite being the perfect Pisces photocopied out of an astrology book, I try to organize and structure myself as much as possible. When one is multi-faith and/or multi-tradition, that's an essential skill. Wanting the stay away as far as possible from what I already know and do, I went on a God quest.

Who did I felt attracted to? Who did I want to "work with"? I didn't know but He already knew. I felt farther than I was at the beginning after checking various mythological websites for inspiration. Out of the sub-final list that I made, I came to the conclusion that I was all over the place literally: too many different pantheons and none of those Gods listed made me strongly resonate. I suspected that the cerebral approach would not do it this time so I quickly went in trance to visit my astral temple. It was April 26 2014 and I wasn't going to… my astral temple.

I found myself in deep trance in what looked like an Olympian steps leading to an unknown sanctuary. I happily climbed them and found a deserted minimalist temple. I was completely naked. A muscular but not totally buff man was waiting for me there. His skin was vibrantly bright and tanned, calling me to touch Him. His hair was curly and shinning blonde. As He got closer to me, I intuited His name: Apollo.

In an intense sexual experience, Apollo entered me. Once ended, we smiled and said "Thank you!" before quickly reintegrating my body.

I wondered what happened to me and why. In the Gaudiya Vaisnava lineage, the taste for romantic love with the Divine is the highest mood but the goal is to assist in the loving pastimes, not to enjoy ourselves. My Hindu orthodoxy was being affected. I had to rethink my cosmology, theology and thealogy. Was this like a "maryaj lwa" in Haitian Vodou? I was later initiated into a male-centered Witchcraft tradition and it all made more sense to me. The God was strangely close to me which surprised me as it's not usually the case for a first-degree initiate to the extent that it was my Lady, the Goddess, who seemed a bit more distant yet ever watching. My sexuality changed greatly and I was trained to act as a channel, a receptacle for the Divine Masculine. I understood that this astral experience had been an initiation, the beginning of a new shift.

I have always ridiculously wanted to be pregnant and give birth to an extent that is not even funny. I was impregnated that night by Apollo and my baby is ever growing: it's my ideal witch and priestly self. It is a continual rebirthing of that Self.

Apollo, my Sun, ever shine of us! You are light, you are life, you are magick.

"As I near the bed,
He smiles and gazes.
Flower-arrows fill the world.
The sport of love,
Its glow and luxuries
Are indescribable, O friend,

And when I yield myself,
His joy is endless.
Freeing my skirt,
He snatches at my garland.
My downcast mind
Is freed of frontiers,
Though my life is held
In the net of his love.
He drinks my lips.
With heart so thrilled,
He take my clothes away.
I lose my body
At his touch
And long to check
But grant his love.
Says Vidyāpati:
Sweet as honey
Is the talk of a girl in love."
(Poem of Vidyāpati (1352? - 1448?), rendered into English by David R. Kinsley)

Ariel Manohara is a Hindu priest of the Gaudiya Vaisnava lineage, a bhakti yogi, and a witch. He is initiated in the Minoan Brotherhood, New York Welsh Traditional Witchcraft, and the priesthood of l'École des mystères de la Déesse (a Goddess-worshipping School and Order active in French-speaking countries). He lives near Montréal, Qc, Canada and works in with autistic young people and in hospice care.

A Priest at Delphi

Foam clings to our lips and shoulders
As the glistening sea creature beckons
Teasing, seducing, drawing us nearer
I can see a beach, rocky outcrops and sand
Divine dream and saline reality have merged
I no longer know where I am, only that I must follow Him
I swim beside my fellow sailors, each stripped naked
Before we dove from the sinking vessel, our livelihood
There is nothing left of our possessions from Krete
All that now lies far below in Poseidon's deep pastures
I hear the laughter of Nereids as we reach the Korinthian surf
They know that we are no longer ordinary men, but servants
We hear thunder, lightning flashes as we crawl onto land
Although the sky is clear and the warm rays of Helios reach us
The Dolphin is gone and before us stands the Glory of Olympos
The Far-Darter raises his hands as serpents lick our ears
Suddenly wind and gull and water have a clear voice
As will the feverish mumblings of the Pythia in trance

Five years have passed, and there are pilgrims each day
Some we must turn away, so they go further up Parnassos
To throw bones, dice and pebbles before the Nymphs
Not all can understand what the Korykian girls reveal
And so they leave believing that their fortunes will turn
Every day is the same, every week, every month
Different faces, true, but the same problems
Even when kings arrive, they are the same
None seem to notice the Maxims inscribed
Even if they are able to read the letters
I think back to before I left Knossos
We knew Apollo there too
He was a pillar who guarded
Our gates and courtyards
But my family roasted
Mountain goats for
The Honey Sweet
Maiden of Dikti

There is no place more beautiful than the heights of Delphi
To watch Helios rise and Helios set, to know the light of Apollo
That shines in the minds of men from all places and walks of life
Maybe I judged some too harshly, but others deserved their fate
A few hurled themselves off cliffs rather than face what we foretold
Merchants, heroes, conquerors, thieves, lovers, I remember them
The Pythia herself still looks as young as when I first arrived
I would think the troubles of the world would have aged her

But she is never herself, only a vessel to store destinies
One day she might awake with Leto's Son gone
She would ask for a doll or run to pick flowers
For like Persephone she was plucked away
Like us
Some say we take bribes from wealthy men
But no coin can change the Will of Zeus
No clashing of bronze shields
No swimming against tides
No breaking of marble

~Leonidas

Leonidas is a high priest in the Minoan Brotherhood. He runs Temenos Gryphon, the only Minoan grove (their name for a coven) in the Washington DC Metro area. In May of 2014, he was able to visit both Delphi and Crete for the first time with his partner, who is also an initiate of the tradition. 'A Priest at Delphi' had been written as a rough draft in January 2010, then edited for this anthology six years later. It was inspired by an intense dream wherein Leonidas was an old man on an airplane flying back to Delphi knowing that he would die there.

My Apollo

My love My healer My deity My hope

Apollo is my light when I am in darkness.

Apollo is my healer when I am sick.

Apollo is my love when I feel alone.

Apollo is God when I need guidance.

So many times in my life, I've felt Apollo around me.

With me. Protecting me. Healing me, physically and mentally.

He is beautiful and caring.

A true God among the Gods.

I'm grateful for Apollo to allow me to ask for his help and that he has been willing to give it when I've asked and, also, when I was not strong enough to ask.

With Love, My Apollo.

~~~Kristin

Kristin is a devotee of the Graeco-Roman Deities, a practicing Witch of Italian descent, and a dedicate mother who makes her home in the Rhode Island area.

Apollo in the Southern Itallic Craft Tradition(s) (Jonathan Sousa)

Caveat: Southern Italian Craft is, in all its forms and sects, an oathbound initiatory system. To that end: No oaths were violated in writing this article.

In Southern Italy, Apollo is (in varying forms) the God with the most prominent following amongst Witches. The most popular Goddess is His sister, Diana. Aside from matching the lunar-solar pairing of modern Neo-Wicca, this preference for Apollo strikes many outside of our Ways as… odd. Per popular NeoPaganism, the God of Witchcraft is a Horned God of fertility, the sun, and the otherworld. And, per the old-time Wica, the Powerful God is Lord of Death and that which lies beyond It. Apollo, per the farce of Classical mythology most are familiar with, is all Light, all Order, all Logic. Yet, in the old Temple ruins, in fragments of lore, He tempts us to dig deeper beyond the gospels of Homer and the epistles of Hesiod. With Apollo, as with Diana, there are deeper, darker Mysteries at work.

Southern Italy was once part of Magna Graecia. There have been more temples discovered for the Hellenic Deities there than in mainland Greece itself. Outside the pale of the Athenian exegesis (which became majority opinion), vestiges of other ways and facets of the Immortals survived.

Per Empedocles, a student of Pythagoroas, Apollo's Sun is formed of fire from the Underworld. And that fire must invariably return to its root and home. This is why, at the end of His mythic journey during the daylight, Apollo enters the Underworld and makes His home with the Daughters of Night. Encompassing the Empyrean heights and Stygian depths, Apollo was the All in All.

The Pythagoreans themselves were heirs of Apollo's oulios priesthood, renowned throughout the ancient world for their skill at dream incubation and healing. This priesthood also were renowned as law-givers to the populus – not the laws of social politicos, but the laws that governed right relationship with all existence. They were immensely practical. And they passed their order down to others in a lineage formalized through ritual adoption.

Throughout Southern Italy, every temple to Apollo that has been found is associated with springs, caves, or chasms. These openings were considered doors to the Underworld. By entering through these gates, one 'died before physical death'. There, in that still ecstasy found in the dark places, Apollo would speak through the sacred silence. Father afield, in Scythia, we find contemporary traditions where Apollo is linked to shamanic practices, journeying upon the wind, and miraculous healing, all by making the darkness conscious in this silence.

It has been noted that this makes Apollo an ecstatic God and savior-figure. As other authorities attest, His ecstasy was neither the frenzy of Dionysos nor the catharsis of the Great Mother. Instead, it was the reverie of deep meditation. By this Art, one could stop the Wheel of Fate and behold all as it truly is. One can not undergo this without being changed. One did not do this for base purposes. One did this to join with the Gods and emerge from the Underworld as a bridge thereto. One did this for the benefit of community.

In these cults, Apollo was typically paired with Hekate and/or Persephone. Per Roman exegesis, these were the terrestial and chthonic faces of Diana Triformis. Yet, amongst the Sicilians and Sardinians, Persephone was the Dread Mistress of All Below and All Above. When Apollo was identified with the Phoenician God Erragal, He was said to have entered the Underworld and wooed Persephone. She crowned Him as Her Mate and Co-ruler there.

Diana reigns in popular lore as the Queen of Witches. Some, drawing too closely upon Her links to Artemis, have posited this was due to sexual politics. This may be. And the reasons why She was and is such are complex, beyond the focus of this article.

Still, it is an important part of Continental Craft theology that our Matron and Patron be both Twins and a mated pair. This is not a place to comment upon sexual liberation. Nor does the Hermetic principle of polarity do it adequate justice. Per an ancient saying, "Where Diana is, Apollo goes. Where Apollo abides, Diana is near."

We can look at this Mystery another way. One of Diana's alternative Names is Iana (Jana). And Apollo was identified – in Neoplatonic theurgy - with Ianus Pater (Janus) as Lord of the Poles and Keeper of the Gates. And, in the rituals of Theurgic ascent, one petitioned Hekate and Ianus for success in the operation(s).

During the Middle Ages, the Roman Church tended to redefine Apollo as the epitomy of order. He was the best of those naughty Pagan Gods. Some even went so far as to see Him as a metaphor for Christ as King. Others, recognizing Diana's more subversive elements, wrote Him down as yet another case of diabolic imitation.

As the various lineages of what we now call Italian Traditional Witchcraft, Apollo has been syncretized with both Jesus Christ and the Devil. He has also been masked by Saint Michael the Archangel – and many of Michael's Italian churches stand on sites long associated to Apollo in His Underworld aspects.

Here we must speak of the mystery of Lucifer. Lucifer was a popular epithet for various Deities and Spirits in the Roman world. It means "The Light bringer." It was also popular as a name for men and women… so much so that there have been at least THREE Saint Lucifers in the rolls of the Catholic and Orthodox church. (That said, the only historically documented one is Saint Lucifer of Cagliari, Sardinia). And, before the Vulgate cemented a more demonic pedigree, Lucifer was used as a title for Jesus Christ himself!

Due to the influence of Gnostic heresy and Hermetic philosophy, Apollo Lucifero came to be seen as a fallen angel. However, His fall was a willing sacrifice to anchor the Light of Spirit in the realm of Matter. He taught that each man, each woman, was their own savior and their own cause of damnation. Our choice defined which aspect predominated. As part of this Fall, He periodically incarnated as various figures, ranging from the Edenic Serpent to Attys to Adonis to Bacchus to Mithra, to Orpheus and Trophonios and Empedocles, and, ultimately, to Jesus of Nazareth.

Specific references to Apollo aside, similar teachings concerning this Luciferian gnosis exist outside of Southern Italian occultism. It had prevalence in France, Ireland, and Spain. It was also articulated in a more modern era by the British occultist, Madeline Montalban. From Montalban's Order of the Morning Star, it passed into some lineages of Traditional Wica, as well as some offshoots of the Golden Dawn. Lady Gwen Thompson, who founded NECTW, and the F(a)eri(e) Tradition articulated by Victor and Cora Anderson, also are recorded as having shared similar teachings.

Apollo's cult amongst the Southern Italian Streghe and Maghi is both a survival and an evolution. And, despite a focus on lesser-known roles, it does not invalidate His more popular aspects as Lord of Light, God of Song, and Divine Healer. Rather it deepens those roles and allows for engaging with Him more fully, as a complex being (just as we ourselves are).

Nota Bene: *I would like to thank the following for assisting with an earlier version of this article, namely by giving advice, pointing me toward resources, and general encouragement: Lori Bruno, Beth Ann Mastromarino, Marie Antonia, Vinnie Russo, Scotti Brancher, Gwendolyn Reece, and Owen Rowley.*

Resources:

Anderson, Cora. 50 Years in the Fairy Tradition.

Artisson, Robin. The Witching Way of the Hollow Hill.

Bonefry, Yves. Roman and European Mythologies.

Evola, Julius, and the UR Group. Introduction to Magic.

Flowers, Stephen. Hermetic Magic.

Ginzburg, Carlo. Ecstasies: Deciphering the Witches' Sabbath.

Hall, Manly P. Secret Teachings of All Ages.

Howard, Michael. Children of Cain.

Johnson, Sarah Illes. Hekate Soteira.

Kingsley, Peter. In the Dark Places of Wisdom.

Leland, Charles. Aradia, or the Gospel of the Witches of Italy.

Martello, Leo. Witchcraft: The Old Religion.

Morgan, Lee. Deed Without a Name.

Rahn, Otto. <u>Lucifer's Court.</u>

Sousa, Jonathan. <u>Reflections in Diana's Mirror.</u>

Theitic & Robert Mathieson. <u>Rede of the Wiccae.</u>

Valiente, Doreen. <u>ABC of Witchcraft.</u>

Poetic Offerings

I

I raise my voice to Apollo,
beloved of the Muses,
shining son of Latona,
Twin and Hidden Face of Diana,
Sire of the Royal Blood
of the Wise and Thrice-Blessed.
You who unleash the plagues,
and bind them at your pleasure.
You who speak with
the tongue of the Goddess Earth,
revealing the Logos of the Aion
to those who love
Justice, and Goodness, and Truth.
You who temper wild passion,
and tempt us to the deeper ecstasy
found in still silence,
down, down, down to heed
the counsels of Those Below.
You who avenge every wrong,
and restore All to primordial harmony,
the Music of the Spheres
upon the lyre
as Mnemosyne's Nine dance
to maintain the Holy Pattern.
You who, hanging in agony
upon the Fourfold Cross,
endured all that we might become as Gods.
Lord of the Maghi,
Goatherd, Dreamer within the Land,
blessed Apollo,
Great Bridegroom, All-seeing Immortal,
Winged Serpent
with coils of living flame -
and inspire us.
Drain away the delusions

that obscure our radiance.
Give us the venom
of Serpent-Mother,
the price and the prize of Wisdom.
Apollo, Lucifero, Pholarkos, Soranus,
in all the holy Names:
I set this paean for you.
May your Spirit be increased,
may these Words nourish you,
may my Love glorify your Names.
So be it ardane!

II

Apollo, Great Python,
whose great clarity
in the Depths of the Underworld
provides the cure for every ill;
Apollo, I offer
my anguish and pain,
my joy and pleasure,
my integrity and my pettiness,
my fear and my courage,
all as instruments of your Light
in the Great Work of Absolute Good.
May those who suffer
find their anguish alleviated
by this offering;
May those who triumph
remember compassion,
crowned by this offering;
May those who wander
have purpose and vision
to renew all worlds
in the perfection
of my sacrifice.

III

The Tripod beckons.
Pythons rise upon my soul.
Still Voice of God.

IV

Engulf me in your flames, O Beloved -
the warmth of your love is all consuming rapture,

it drowns my Soul and I ascend.
There, at the precipice of seven steps,
having climbed, crawling forth like Proserpine,
I reach and am caught.
O Shining Lord, Savior, Groom Divine,
my heart pours with yours
to fill the grael of our marriage bed.
In the throws of surrender, your horned mask
is torn off and reveals:
under a harsh face of Judgement
lies all-merciful light,
ceaseless tears to drown even the flaming pit
and restore Earth to paradise.

~ Jonathan Sousa

Litany of Apollon Musegetes

(For inspiration and illumination)

***

In the Good, the Just, and the Beautiful, I set these words for you, Apollo, God who inspires as a firebrand cast out upon the world, consuming all in creativity and beauty. Your lyre maintains the cosmic song. O Beloved of Memory, Prince of Song, Master of Incantations, Dreaming Prophet that is Rootless Root of Artistry – lead the Nine Daughters of Mnemosyne from Mount Parnassus to crown us with your living light. May that same light carry us ever forward upon the Way of Return.

+++

Calliope, Muse of Epics and Sagas, may the river of memory feed the Heroic Soul within us.

Clio, Muse of History, help us to reconcile the past, the present, and the future, in telling our tale.

Euterpe, Muse of Song and Dance, whose eulogies honor those whose deeds have touched our lives with the better, open us to the song and dance of life.

Erato, Muse of that which compels, seduces, and persuades, help us to captivate attention and wield it for noble ends.

Melpomene, Muse of Tragedy, help us to cultivate emotion.

Polyhymnia, Muse of Many Hymns, let our works honor the Gods above, below, around, and within.

Thalia, Muse of Comedy, help us to laugh at and learn from our mistakes, using them to better our Selves and our Peoples.

Ourania, Muse of the Stellar Regions, grant us some measure of your numinous grace.

+++

Daughters of Memory, with laurel-crowned Apollo, may gnosis (knowledge) and charis (grace) indwell us. May your pneuma (spirit) set us aflame to express All for the highest and the best. May we give form to Beauty here! Esti ei nai!

~ Jonathan Sousa

A Dinner Date with Apollo *(Jonathan Sousa)*

The seeds of this article are threefold: Rituals from the PGM to gain a *Pahedros* (Divine Follower) i.e. a familiar spirit from the ranks of the daimones; the concept of sacrifice as a formal meal linking deity and worshipper by the codes of hospitality; and the concept of courting the Gods in order to know Them better and involve Them in our lives. Additionally, in the Craft tradition I follow, our Gods are viewed and treated as Family: we include Them in our meals. Lastly, elements of Crowley's Liber Astarte have inspired some of my suggestions.

The goal is to devote an evening to the God, where everything is both an offering to Him and a sharing of your Life with Him. It is tempting to paint it as a romantic rendezvous, but one can also see it as a weekly/monthly dinner with a dear friend or as analogous to the traditional Jewish keeping of Sabbath.

If you feel drawn Apollo and wish to feel closer to Him, this is a proven technique. If you wish to thank Apollo for help in a private matter or otherwise offer Him a place in your life, this is a most capable votive act. If you are claimed by Apollo as a Godspouse, this is a phenomenal way of honoring that bond. If you have a request or are seeking a dream oracle, this is a traditional way to seek your answers.

(Incidentally, one can adapt this for the worship of any Deity or Spirit.)

At its simplest level, this entails preparing a meal and enjoying it in a sacred manner. You may want to set a place for Apollo at your dining table, or set up a dining area in your temple space. The menu may be whatever you are inspired to make. You may include poetry and music, incense and candles, flowers and dancing, as you will. In the end, what truly matters is that you break bread and make time and space for connection thereby. The following rubric and menu are suggestions only, based on my own praxis. I hope they inspire your own creativity and piety.

Caveat: Per some factions, this praxis is an expression of hubris. I acknowledge that such may be the case in a very fundamentalist, kray-kray, paranoid reading of the lore. However, I am neither a reconstructionist nor a zealot. I am a Traditionalist Witch and, per the dictates and customs of that path, this is a proper expression of personal piety.

An Outline of Service:

I. Clean your house, not just your ritual/dining area. Then, purify the house and seal it as per your tradition. The ancient Greeks would most likely sprinkle *khernips* (water made holy by the addition of salt, sulphur, or a lit ember into its water) and burn frankincense.

II. Make an offering of bread to ALL the Gods, Goddesses, and Spirits of your household. This insures peace amongst all your commitments thereto.

III. Prepare a "seat of honor" for Apollo, either in your dining room, common area, bedroom, or your temple space. (In my praxis, I pay special attention to a placement at the table, but bring a small statue of Him throughout my home in each stage).

IV. Set everything in order. Refocus on your intent (i.e. devotion, petition, seeking guidance, gratitude, etc). Formally invite and welcome Apollo as an honored guest into your home.

V. Prepare the food. I usually describe each ingredient to the God and/or describe the inspiration for the recipe. During this time, I may also recite poetry (my own, the Orphic hymns, and/or the Homeric hymns), play music I deem appropriate, or share drinks and snacks (i.e. a glass of wine or cup of tea with freshly sliced melon), as well as meditating upon the God's attributes.

VI. The Meal. I make it a point to serve Apollo first as my guest and loved one. Then, I will serve myself. I usually prefer the only illumination to be via candlelight or oil lamps. As I sit down, I will bless the food in Apollo's name. As I eat, I will talk to the God extemporaneously, emptying my heart and mind. Nothing is too small or too big. I will share my fears and my hopes, my challenges and my triumphs. I will usually allow for moments of silence. Sometimes I have been surprised with epiphanies, insights, and other signs of the God's response. Other times... there is a warm glow of sharing in nonverbal ways.

VII. Particulars: If I am expressing gratitude for a miracle, I will dedicate the meal to that purpose. If I need help or am seeking a dream oracle, I will make that request and meditate upon it. If this is a purely votive act, I will simply offer Him my love.

VIII. Contemplation and mutual enjoyment. I may dance, recite more poetry, or otherwise entertain the God as I would a beloved guest in my home.

IX. Closing: I would thank the God for attending and request that, as I re-entered more mundane space and time, there be peace, truth, and love between us. I would also thank the Household Guardians and other Spirits thereof for maintaining peace and allowing the rite to take place.

X. Clean-Up.

Menu Suggestions:

Starters:
Cheese, fresh fruit, nuts (almonds and walnuts in particular).

Beverages: *Wine, Meade, Fruit Juices, Herbal Tea.*

First Course:
Kalamata Olives (pitted and chopped), blended with goat cheese and honey. Spread this over lavash or pita bread. Serve with taboule.

Second Course:

Roasted vegetables seasoned with olive oil, bay laurel, corriander, and garlic.
(I have found that Apollo REALY enjoys a blend of beets, parsnips, and carrots).

Third Course:
Butternut squash and apple soup, seasoned with butter, salt, and pepper.

(Those who allow meat in their diet may serve lamb stew, a roast, or a baked fish, with sweet potato).

Fourth Course:
Blended Greek yogurt, mint leaves, and chopped cucumber.

Dessert:
Baklava or a spicy cake, served with coffee or black tea.

Nota Bene: I would like to thank Lori Bruno, Dawn Adamo Corey, and Vincent Russo for inspiring or otherwise assisting me in creating these recipes.

Jonathan Sousa is a priest(ess) of both Diana and Apollo. He serves these Deities through the initiatory framework of the Italian-American Traditionalist Craft. A published author, he lives in MA.

A Pythia's Prayer

Flay me like Marsyas, make me hollow,
So I may sing your prophecies, Lord of Light.
Strip my refinements, make me callow,
Flay me like Marsyas.

Release me from bondage, let my soul take flight.
Make me your instrument, Lord Apollo.
I long to surrender to your power, bright.

Great Phoibos, lead me and I will follow.
Play me, your flute, bless us with your foresight.
I am my sacrifice and your hallow.
Flay me like Marsyas.

~Gwendolyn Reece

Prayer to Apollon Hyperboreios for Theophania

Come back to us, Lord Apollon, riding upon your sacred swan.
From far beyond the Northern Wind, we call you back, O' Lord of Light.
Io Paian. Io Paian. Io Paian. Io Paian.

With heavy hearts we've waited long and kept your house while you were gone.
We long to hear your holy song and gaze upon your Being, bright.
Come back to us, Lord Apollon, riding upon your sacred swan.

Your house is decked with Daphne, pure; we've clothed your holy xoanon.
With love and hope we wait for you, your sacred flame we feed each night.
Io Paian. Io Paian. Io Paian. Io Paian.

We watch for signs the time has come and wait for you by light of dawn.
Kastilia awakens now; her waters sing her soul's delight.
Come back to us, Lord Apollon, riding upon your sacred swan.

At Didyma they hurt your priests; through Christian night you have withdrawn.
The feast for your return is laid; the omens show the time is right.
Io Paian. Io Paian. Io Paian. Io Paian.

Your Pythia awaits your grace, seated within your adyton.
Please speak with us, great loving God; your counsels share, O' Lord of Light.
Come back to us, Lord Apollon, riding upon your sacred swan.
Io Paian. Io Paian. Io Paian. Io Paian.

~Gwendolyn Reece

Curse-Breaking and Clearing of *Miasma* Ritual for Athena Themis and Apollon Moiragetes (Gwendolyn Reece)

Athena and Apollon

Two of the Olympian deities who exhibit tremendous concern for humanity and the spiritual evolution of both individual humans and human civilization are Apollon and Athena. Athena is the most common patron of the *polis*, which is the community that is beyond the family, and Apollon is revered as the Lawgiver. Important political documents, (such as constitutions and treaties), as well as significant changes in policy, (such as the reforms of Cleisthenes which led to democracy), were taken to the oracles of Apollon for revision and divine sanction by the God of Light. In the Hellenic system, Light is synonymous with Truth.

Themis, as a concept, means "Right Order." True Justice is Right Order. Themis is how reality functions when all of the beings that make up our interdependent cosmos are interacting and inter-relating appropriately, including relationships between humans and each other, humans and the natural world, and humans and the gods and spirits. In many ways, Themis is similar to the Indian concept of *dharma*. Apollon, as the pre-eminent prophetic god and the Lord of Light/Truth, has the full view of Themis and directly counsels humans so that they may make the best choices in their actions. Oracular consultations with Apollon are always about potential actions and include counsel. Moira, often translated as Fate, is causation as it exists within a dramatically interdependent reality. Apollon sees Moira clearly and gives advice about how to act in Light of Moira. One of his forms is as Apollon Moiragetes, which is "Leader of the Moira," which might be translated into Leader of Fate because seeing Moira clearly, He knows how to alter causal chains, changing Fate. Only Apollon and Zeus are ever given this epithet.

Much of the counsel given by Apollon is about how to cleanse *miasma*. *Miasma* is a type of spiritual pollution that occurs when we get out of right relationship, be it right relationship with others, with nature, with the gods, or with ourselves. Cleansing or purifying *miasma* is an incredibly important form of healing because it actually heals our soul-trajectory. It interrupts the flow of cause and effect when we have gotten out of right relationship and realigns it. One of the things that was most surprising to me when I began serving Apollon in rebirthing His oracular cult is that His mantic work is an expression of His healing and vice versa. I had not previously understood that they are two faces of the same thing. His extraordinary compassion is overwhelming and ineffably beautiful. Apollon directly intervenes with humans to give us counsel so that we may purify *miasma* and restore Themis.

Athena can be viewed as the Goddess of Humanity. She is, of course, the Goddess of Wisdom, but She is also the preeminent Hellenic Great One who takes something that is natural and turns it into something that is human. So, for example, both She and Poseidon are deities of the horse, but Poseidon created horses while it was Athena who created the bridle and the chariot. She is the foremost deity associated with human institutions and many of Her forms are abstracted human virtues, such as Justice, Victory, Temperance and so forth. This is why we tend to abstract virtues into female forms. Many of the goddesses, such as Themis, were originally epithets and forms of Athena. Therefore, Athena Themis is the Goddess of Right Order from a human perspective, both individual and communal.

Ritual Intention

This ritual was first offered at the Between the Worlds/Sacred Space Conference of 2015. The intention of this ritual is to break any curses that the practitioner may have laid in a past incarnation that are still active. Themis is eternal and all of reality is interdependent. However, our social understandings of Justice vary across time and cultures. Cursing is often considered an instrument of Justice and, in fact, is often the only instrument of Justice available to those in disempowered positions. As such, those of us who have been magical practitioners for numerous incarnations have probably cast curses that may still be active. Many magical lines are bogged down in old curses that have not fully expired or played out which can end up crippling magical practitioners and our ability to be effective. Part of the problem stems from the fact that it was not uncommon to curse individuals and their lines of descendants. In my work, I have discovered curses that were cast and then the lines intermarried some number of generations later, so the practitioner ended up cursing their own lines. All of this is worthy of a Greek tragedy. It was also not uncommon for curses to be given a time frame that means virtually forever (10,000 years it not atypical). From our contemporary perspective, much of this now seems inappropriate. For those spells that we cast that are still ongoing, we are tied to them in some way and may also have *miasma* as a result. In my understanding, this kind of curse-breaking is something that Apollon and Athena want us to do. They do not want us to guilt-trip or feel badly about what we may or may not have done in the past. They do want us to understand where our hearts and sense of Justice are now and to break any patterns that we would not want to see ongoing.

Mythic Frame of the Ritual

Part of the mythic energy and frame that is being tapped in this ritual is inspired by the play, *The Eumenides*, written by Aeschylus/Aischylos. In this play, Orestes is standing trial before the first jury in the very first court organized by Athena. Orestes is on trial because he avenged himself upon his father's murderer, as was required according to the rules of blood vengeance, but his father's murderer was his own mother. His family was laboring under a series of curses in which the requirements of vengeance cycled from one generation to the next through the House of Atreus, his hereditary line. The Erinyes, the Furies, who are the spirits who upheld the ancient ways of vengeance, act as prosecutor. Apollon acts as the defense attorney and makes the case for the rule of Law over the rule of vengeance. The resolution of the play results in several important outcomes. Athena casts the deciding vote when the jury is split and Orestes is acquitted. This act breaks the cycle of vengeance while simultaneously breaking a long-standing familial curse, releasing the heredity line from *miasma*. It establishes and legitimates the rule of Law over tribalism. Athena further transforms the ancient spirits of vengeance into protective spirits of the *polis*, and renames them the Eumenides. Therefore, this myth fundamentally transforms not just human relations and communities, but also the gods themselves.

Magical Techniques and Information

Curse Anatomy

Curses must have both a powerful thought form and a power source that keeps it going. There are many strategies for breaking curses, but in this instance, what we focus on is breaking the link between the thought form and the power source. Because it is within the structure of the human mind to loop on ideas, words, or visions, which gives energy, it is better in this instance NOT to see or know the specifics about any curse you are striving to break, lest you unintentionally begin powering it by dwelling on it. Therefore, in this ritual we are using the type of psychic abilities that Ivo Dominguez Jr. has dubbed the "noirs," specifically automatic writing. During the ritual, a guided meditation is used to capture and inscribe the link between the thought form and the power source onto a piece of pottery so that it becomes embodied. Allow yourself to do the work at the level of the subconscious. Know that you have done it effectively. Have confidence in yourself.

Dragon Breath

After the link is embodied, it is important to switch gears from a very calm, receptive, passive mode to active will. For this, use dragon breathing by inhaling a deep belly breath and then rapidly forcing out eight short bursts of breath. Please note, this technique is contraindicated for high blood pressure and if you feel light headed, sit down immediately. If you know you are likely to have issues with the Dragon Breath, please use deep belly breathing whilst focusing on awakening and enlivening the solar plexus and transpersonal chakras.

The Tools

The use of the pottery (I recommend clay saucers of the type used for small terracotta flower pots) as an embodied vehicle for inscribing the energetic link ties the working to the first court of Athens. The early Athenian courts used either pebbles or pottery shards to mark votes and they used pottery shards that were inscribed for the *ostraka*, which is when they decided to cast a citizen out of the city (ostracism). Therefore in creating the pottery shards in this ritual, we are recalling one of the ways of lawfully casting out a baneful influence. The Gavel of Themis is a gavel. Mine was an actual judge's gavel that had been used on the bench and is consecrated to Athena Themis. The Gavel of Themis is used to break the link that was keeping the curse alive, thereby restoring Right Order. The two different receptacles, one black and one white, recalls the ways in which votes were collected in the Athenian courts and also serves to split the pieces of the curse from each other.

Breaking the Curse

Focus on your power and intention. Lay the pottery down on the board that will be the platform for breaking the curse. Lay the veil on top of it. Pick up the Gavel of Themis, know you are restoring Right Order and purifying *miasma*. Break the pottery. The reason for the veil is to signify that you are breaking both visible and invisible patterns as well as keeping the shards from flying and hurting anyone.

Chants

- "Salt and Water" by Gwendolyn Reece
  http://www.ivodominguezjr.com/Panpipes_Pagan_Chant_Site/chants/salt-and-water.html
- "Full Blessed Children" [Source Unknown]
- "May the Circle Be Open" [Adapted from Starhawk]

Materials Needed:

- Small table and cloth for altar
- Statue of Athena Themis

- Statue of Apollon
- Candle
- Two receptacles for pot shards (preferably one black and one white)
- Pottery saucers (one per person)
- Markers (one per person)
- Gavel of Themis
- Platform for breaking the pottery (a hard board)
- Veil to cover the pottery before hammering
- Bowl for salt water
- Salt and water
- Incense thurible
- Incense (preferably bay laurel based)
- Copies of ritual

Ritual Outline

Magical Aims of the Ritual: To enable practitioners to break cycles of vengeance by rupturing the link between the power-source and thought-form of a curse. In this instance, for this group ritual, we will focus on clearing any curses cast BY us in past incarnations. This ritual relies heavily on the psychic skills that Ivo Dominguez Jr has dubbed the "noirs," namely, those that operate below the threshold of consciousness. Even if you have the ability to bring the thought forms to direct consciousness through various other skills, for the purposes of this ritual, it is inadvisable that you do so, due to the propensity of the mind to loop on narrative and image, which is a power-source for forms. It would, therefore, be antithetical to the intention.

1. Grounding and Centering
2. Purification of Participants and Space:
   a. Chant: *Salt and water, cleanse this space, open us to receive grace. Purge the air of all the bane, purge our spirits of the same. We come before the temple gate, full of love and purged of hate.*
3. Cast the Circle
4. Call to Athena Themis and Apollon Moiragetes

Athena Themis, Pallas Athena, Goddess of Wisdom, hear me! Know me! Great One, answer my call! Glaukopis, Boulaia, Themis, Bright Counselor, Upholder of Right Order, I call to you today and ask you to join this holy rite, dedicated to doing the work you desire. Athena Themis, you maintain the ideals of Right Order in the Kosmos, and help us manifest and restore it on Earth, for that is what Justice is. Compassionate One through your wisdom you transformed the Erinyes, the Furies into the Kindly Ones and taught us how to break the cycles of vengeance. Today, we, a cadre of Magical beings, come before you, standing in our power, determined to break and rend asunder any thought forms we have created that maintain these baneful cycles and to manifest Right Order in this world, in our lives, and in our relations. We come to serve compassion, evolution, and growth. We ask for your assistance in this rite. Help us do the work that needs to be done, and protect us during this rite and afterwards. Thank you, Bright One. I bid you Hail and Welcome.

Phoibos Apollon, Moiragetes, Shining One, Lord of Light, of Enlightenment, of Truth, hear me and know me! Know the love and dedication in my heart, and answer my call, Bright Lord. Apollon, I call to you this day and ask you to join this holy rite. Apollon Alexikakos, averter of all evil, Great One, we honor you as the one who broke the self-perpetuating cycles of guilt. Apollon Maleatas, Physician of Souls, Great Compassionate One, over and over again, through your counsel and your oracles you have given those who have grown and have regret the ways and means to cleanse ourselves and heal from *miasma*, the spiritual pollution from having done wrong. Today, we join together, to end and cleanse any actions from the past that continue to create harm--harm to ourselves or to others. We come to serve compassion, evolution, and growth. We ask for your assistance in this rite. Help us do the work that needs to be done, purify us and protect us during this rite and afterwards. Thank you, blessed and loving Apollon. I bid you Hail and Welcome

5. Invocation of our own God-Forms

Invocation of Our Own God-Forms - Focus your attention in your head, move the point of consciousness deep into your brain, about two inches below where the plates in your skull meet. Now send your attention up, through the crack in the plates of your skull, up, until your center of consciousness is about one foot above your physical skull. Feel it fill with the Light of your being, drawing from your heart, and feel it become a beacon. In your mind, call, to the God you will someday be, for that Fate is inevitably yours and in that aspect of Beingness, Time does not exist. Call. Call. O Great One Who is Me, I call to you! Please, come and fill this vessel and help me do the work of bringing Light and Love into manifestation on this Earth. Please help me to end any workings that are not in accordance with you. Please come, come, and be present.

6. Exclamation of Intent [Call and Response]

Priest/ess: Magicians, you stand in your power before the Great Ones, why have you come?

All: To break the cycles of vengeance, to end the cycles of destruction, to rend asunder any work from the past that now inhibits spiritual evolution…mine or another's.

Priest/ess: How will you do this?

All: I will find the link between the form and its animating life-force and impress it into manifested form, to be broken

Priest/ess: And this you will do. It is within your power, it is within your competence, and it is your will to do this work.

7. Scribing and Manifesting the Link Between the Power Source and Thought Form. *Guided Meditation and scribing activity*

Guided Meditation - Take the clay, the form into which you will impress the link into in your non-dominant hand and take the pen in your other. Relax. Breathe deeply and relax. Let go of all your preconceived notions…of all ideas…of what anything should look or feel like and just relax into your body. Fully relaxed, you are drifting down, down, down into darkness where there is no sight. It is like lying under a moonless and starless night. Soft, dark, and welcoming. We are going to take three deep breaths, and with each breath, relax your body, going even deeper. Relax. Relax. Relax. We are going to take three more deep breaths and relax our minds, going even deeper. Relax. Relax. Relax. I am going to count down from ten and, with each count, you are going to become more and more relaxed. [Count down]. You are now in a state of total relaxation. You are in a place of allowing. Allowing your deeper self that is in the darkness--your deeper knowledge, to be present, deep, deep in the dark. Now I am speaking to the you that knows with your deep conscious…your deep knowing. Deep self, if there is any piece of magic that is still active and not in accord with your evolution or ideals, find it. Find it and find the link between the power source and the form. Now, deep self, use the pen, and push that link onto the clay in your hands. Embody the link that is there. Impress the link into the clay so that it now exists in the manifested world. Thank you, deeper self, thank you for transforming the clay and making manifest the link we need to break. Thank you. We are now going to come back to full consciousness. The dark is lightening, like a sunrise…subtle at first, but with the light increasing.

We become more and more alert until we return fully and completely, still in our power and we know that the key to breaking the form is manifested in the clay in our hands.

8. Shift Energy to Active Will

    Dragon Breathing: SAFETY NOTE – this is contraindicated for cardiac conditions or high blood pressure. If you feel light headed, SIT DOWN.[1]

9. Exclamation of Intent [Call and Response]

Priest/ess: Magicians, you hold in your hands the link between baneful form and the power that keeps it alive. What is your intent?

All: To break the cycles of vengeance, to end the cycles of destruction, to rend asunder any work from the past that now inhibits spiritual evolution…mine or another's.

Priest/ess: How will you do this?

All: We will take the Gavel of Themis, and destroy the form that keeps the bane alive.

Priest/ess: Is this within your power?

All: Yes, it is within my power

Priest/ess: Is this within your competence?

All: Yes, it is within my competence

Priest/ess: Is this in alignment with your True Will?

All: Yes, it is in alignment with my True Will

Priest/ess: Then proceed in this Sacred Work, and support each other in its fulfillment. May all the cycles of vengeance be broken and rent asunder.

10. Charge the Gavel of Themis: Pass the gavel around the circle. Each person holds it, charges it, and says, **"Here among us is the Gavel of Themis."**

11. Breaking the link
    a. Chant - spoken: *May all the cycles of vengeance be broken [3x]; Break, break and be Dispelled.*
    b. One at a time, as you feel moved, bring your pottery, embodying the link, to the altar. Stand before Athena Themis and Apollon Moiragetes, reinforce your connection to your

---

[1] You may substitute belly breathing, while focusing on activating both the transpersonal and solar plexus.

own God-self, lay the pottery on the altar, cover it with the veil, take up the consecrated gavel, and use it to break to clay. Take the pieces and put some into each receptacle, separating the pieces.

12. Prayer for Integration and Protection: *Place your hands on your crown, and run your hands down your body, stopping at the belly. Hold your hands on your belly and lock in the protection and integration.*

Prayer for Integration and Protection

Great Ones, Athena Themis, Apollon Moiragetes, we ask for your assistance. May we and all affected parties of this work safely integrate the release and the breaking of patterns. Please protect and assist us in this integration. We call to our own God-selves, ensure that we are protected and that we integrate the shifting patterns of this release for our own higher good and for the good of all beings. So mote it be.

13. Chant: We have all that we need
We Have All That We Need
Full Blessed Children Of Space
Light Shines Full On Our Faces
Bringing Love, Illumination, P e a c e ...

14. Thank the Deities, including our own God-Selves

To our own God-selves, thank you for being present. Thank you for a glimpse of our own true splendor. Help us maintain and strengthen the conscious connection to you. Help us clarify, purify and strengthen our natures so that our divinity can shine through our forms and let us walk as blessings on this earth. Please remain present and help us know your voice and understand your guidance. Thank you.

Athena Themis, Great Goddess of Justice, thank you for being present in this rite. Thank you for guiding us, for strengthening our ability to trust ourselves, and helping us hold the space for each other to do this important work. Great One, we ask for your continued blessing, guidance and protection as we integrate this working and serve the world by being who we are supposed to be. Thank you Athena

Themis. We bid you Hail and Farewell.

Phoibos Apollon Moiragetes, Lord of Light and Averter of All Evil, thank you for being present in this rite. Thank you for guiding us, for strengthening our ability to trust ourselves, and helping us hold the space for each other to do this important work. Great One, we ask for your continued blessing, guidance and protection as we integrate this working and serve the world by being who we are supposed to be. Thank you Phoibos Apollon. We bid you Hail and Farewell.

15. Close the Circle

16. Chant: *May the Circle be Open, but Unbroken. May the Love of the Old Ones be ever in your heart. Merry Meet, And Merry Part, And Merry Meet Again.*

Biography

Gwendolyn Reece - A modern witch, Theosophist, and Neoplatonist, Gwendolyn has been devoted to the Hellenic deities, especially Athena and Apollon, since roughly Mycenaean times. She serves Them within the nation's capital as a priestess of the Theophania Temple of Athena and Apollon. She found and recognized a place for herself in contemporary Paganism in the mid-1980s and has called herself a Witch ever since. She is a member of the Assembly of the Sacred Wheel and is a graduate of Caroline Kenner's shamanic apprenticeship program through the Gryphon's Grove School of Shamanism. She has lectured extensively for the Theosophical Society for 14 years and has held multiple leadership positions within the society. She serves as President of the Sacred Space Foundation and has served on the Board of Directors for Cherry Hill Seminary. Gwendolyn is on the faculty of American University. In addition to her work as a practitioner, she uses her academic position to conduct research on contemporary Paganism with the intention of both furthering the scholarly discourse and providing useful information back to Pagan communities.

Dancing with the lord of Light

(M'aat De Montrond)

In the fall of 2005 I was watching my WiccanHigh priestess Mary Chapman perform with her belly dance troupe The Moon Goddess Caravan (Folsom, CA). They were doing a performance at the local metaphysical shop Planet Earth Rising.

During the second Saturday market I saw the light that evening as the sun was setting. I felt like I had just saw my future flash right before my eyes. I was only eighteen and at the start of my journey into life.

My teacher Mary insisted that I learn how to dance, to honor her first teacher in the art, as well as to increase the visibility of male artists. To her, dancing was the cure for everything. It's an old Sicilian thing, that dancing can heal.

That is true. And, through the dance, Apollo taught me how to heal my own inner daemons. I felt like he was saying it's time to heal my son and let your light shine for nobody but you.

During the process, I had learned from other teachers in the community, of traditional belly dance from my long time childhood friend who use to groom my old Airedale dog Houston. She was like a second mother to me, Tina Anderson. She and the Ottoman traders they had a flare for getting the parties started at the Renaissance fairs. Those summer and Fall days were like being back in the medieval ages and I felt my light shine from a different past life.

As Apollo shown his light over the year,I had gone through many metamorphoses, let alone my evolution as a belly dancer. I had performed many times with the troupes. I was also going through a harsh break up at the time.

Apollo had turned into a darker shade of light the shadow that needed to heal my own inner daemons. I gave my battle cry and I found the darker side of Apollo's light. I started to understand what my soul needed. It wanted a new sound to move to but a sound that could heal this darkness.

One night during the summer of 2006 me and my girlfriends Red Amy and Shy(Shira) were at a local coffee shop getting something to drink. A local belly dance tribal fusion troupe known as Unmata from hot pot studios was to perform there in that night's show case.

We were entranced by their dance and this style which is called tribal fusion belly dance it was beautiful but as the lights went out the darkness in me felt like it started to heal…Apollon had came to me!

As the leader Amy Sigil of Unmata came out, I saw a light bright that night I could see her light shining so bright that night that this was a style of dance that I would be drawn to work with to heal myself. As I was healing through the time I was spending most of my Sunday nights at the local Goth Club the Asylum. I was finding my own light healing in the shadows that felt like I was right at home for once I never felt alone again. A friend and dear teacher Raven Digitalis taught me the way of the Goth Music could help me heal those scars that need to be brought to the light I felt right. So as my love grew for the Goth scene and culture I started to fall into a beautiful Abyss of music that would heal me. The voices of Industrial, EBM(Electronic body music)Goth, Pagan Folk, opera, classical cello and 80 new wave.

I just started to make my body move into a trance possessed state of mind. I was able to finally be free and to love myself again. Apollo had shown me to take whatever it is you need to heal and dance through the darkness into the dawn. As I have always said what's in your blood is in your blood and I felt like I had heard the distant voices of my Greek and Italian ancestors to just keep dancing and I did.

Apollo had blessed me with many performances I had done with my first troupe Mort'e Manifesto (Death Manifested) which was my dark fusion belly dance group I had formed for a while we had did a few shows and some local ones in the bay area of San Francisco dancing for a friends band back in 2010 at the club the DNA lounge I had danced for a few of my favorite local Goth band Mankind is Obsolete and the electronic band William Control we had the stage shinning that night and Apollo made me feel like a star.

As I had danced with Apollo, I was out on a journey to learn the art of dancing and to keep growing. As years had gone by I had reconnected with my old friend Shy and she had introduced me to Hot Pot Studios fusion dancing. I was interested to see where she had grown her roots with Unmata and Hot pot studios I felt like I was in a tribe of wild dancers. As my curiosity grew for fusion dancing I had started to learn some fusion dancing from Shy and another teacher Natasha Storms from hot pots troupe Verbatim. She had taken me under her wing and shown me what the Hot pot was all about. It was hard work to get myself back into shape.

Once I was out on a dark autumn night of 2014, I felt like I had embraced everything. Flowing on the dance floor at the Goth club called Death Guild that I had been attending here and there out of the years. I had stumbled upon a new teacher someone I felt who could show me the way. Her name was Ariellah of Darker Still studios and a belly dance superstar!

She had been a Dark fusion dancer for years. I had always heard of her until she was in front of me as real as the Hindu goddess dark mother Kali Ma. She embraced me and I felt like a shy little boy who's at his first day of school and you see this beam of light her dance moves were so healing to me, I had this light finally erupt in my soul I felt like I had met somebody that understood my dance and my song of the shadows and the sorrows of my own self to heal.

If Apollo had not shown me his light eleven years ago with my path to dancing I don't know where I would have been able to heal if it wasn't for his light healing me on this amazing journey.

As one of his mottoes goes "Know Thyself"... I know who I am , a proud dancer in the light of Apollo.

It is said Apollo loves young men who are talented. I feel that this is true. As my High Priestess Lady Luna would say, "Between the worlds will dance this night with shadow lovers and dark delight....Timeless" (Lady Luna, the Witches Ball)

Blood of Hyacinth

As I saw him that day he was looking at me,
all we could do was stare at each other and share our hearts.
You knew I was your god and you my mortal man a piece of art,
true love comes from the heart that is where real starts.

Like my sister Artemis's wild forest
who is dark we will run now into this abyss,
I did not know my love you were hit in the head with a disk,
by a jealous wind god blowing his cursing kiss.

All I wanted was his mortal kiss,
how did we end up like this.
All I wanted was his last kiss my one last wish.
Hit in the head
now he lays lying dead in a grass that is blood red.
Your spirit is immortal
I will create a flower from our love and blood.
Now the world will see the beautiful flower
from your flesh I created thee!

Blood of Hyacinth
you smell sweet to me
you set my soul free
every time I smell you
it will bring back only loving memories of you and I.

~ Ma'at de Montrond

The poem is dedicated to the memory of Apollo and his mortal lover Hyacinth in the memory of all LGBT humanity who have loved and lost and to always to stop and smell the flowers that love never dies no matter what its our hearts the greatest light Apollo could bless us with.

M'aat De Montrond
Hereditary Witch,Priest, Tarot Reader and belly dancer. M'aat's interest and studies covers a wide range from his ancestral witchcraft practices. His studies and background include: Stregheria (Italian Witchcraft), Afro-Diasporic traditions (Santeria and Vodoun), as well as a draw to where the magic all began from his Greek ancestors and the Hellenistic tradition.

The Lords of Light: Christ and Apollo in Italian Witchcraft

(Dominick Guerriero, Feast of Pentecost, 2016)

Modern pagans are sometimes confused by the dual religious observance of the Italian practitioners of the Craft. It's puzzling to them as to how we can pray the rosary, make bargains with the saints, and give homage to Diana and Proserpina in the same spiritual context.

Our Italian ancestors were extremely pragmatic and practical. As in other regions of the world, syncretism occurred between the old gods and the saints of the newer religion of Christianity.

Also within the catacombs of the early Christians in Rome, we see depictions of pagan deities and heroes such as Helios and Orpheus, alongside that of Christ. A lot of the practices of Roman paganism were preserved in the early rituals of Christianity as it became a religion of converted Gentiles more so than that of Jewish converts. The Church itself adapted many pagan rituals and symbols for its own use as is well documented in its early history. The early Church fathers themselves drew many parallels between the pagan philosophies of Greece and Rome and their own religion. The Greek god most associated with the wisdom and logic of the ancient philosophies was Apollo and in the early centuries of Christianity, both Pagans and Christians saw similarities between Jesus and Apollo. The early Christian fathers also adopted the term Logos from Greek philosophy as a title of Christ. The term Logos meant utterance, speech, reason, as well as the creative principle of the Cosmos. The Logos became identified with Christ as the Word of God.

On the Catholic feast of the Ascension of Christ in May 2016, a day celebrated by the Church as the commemoration of Jesus' triumphal entrance to Heaven, I witnessed a validation of my personal dual-religious observance. After attending the Mass at my local parish, I went across the street to a café for breakfast. In the parking lot of the café was a van with the logo, Apollo: Plumbing and Heating with an image of the Greek god next to the logo. This company was also located in Astoria, NY which is a neighborhood with a large population of Greek immigrants and Americans of Greek descent.

I laughed to myself when I saw the image of Apollo after I had just celebrated a Catholic feast that is considered important in the folk magic traditions of Catholic Italians. This was the inspiration for my writing of this article. How witches of the Italian Craft can honor the Lord of Light whether we call him Jesus Christ, the Son of God or Apollo, the son of Jove. Participating in a Catholic Mass and witnessing in image of Apollo almost directly after, felt like a validation of my spiritual experience as a dual-religious observer of both Catholicism and the Craft.

What then is the connection between Jesus Christ and the god Apollo and how did the two become identified with each other in the minds of both Christians and Pagans?

Throughout the Bible, solar imagery is associated with Christ from the prophet Malachi, an Old Testament prophet who predicted the coming as the Messiah to the appearance of Christ in the Book of Revelations as a powerful monarch whose "face was like the sun shining in its full strength." (Yeoman's)

Christ in the Gospels refers to himself as "The Light of the World." In the event of the Transfiguration wherein Christ reveals his divinity to three of his closest disciples and just as his appearance in the Book of Revelation, "his face shone like the sun, and his garments became white as light." Therefore the solar imagery of Christ is consistent throughout both the Gospels and the Book of Revelations. (Murdoch)

Malachi refers to the Messiah as the Sun of Righteousness, who arises with healing in his wings.

Apollo in the Greco-Roman world was a god of healing and medicine. Jesus also performs many healing miracles during his ministry.

The early Christians who were most likely pagan converts most likely drew parallels between Christ and Apollo in their imagination due to their similar solar attributes. Christ in early Christian art also is depicted as having similar features and attributes to Apollo. These early depictions of Christ are not the bearded savior we are familiar with today but rather a Hellenized version.

"Thus the early images of Christ portray a young, beardless man who bears a strong resemblance to the god Apollo of the Greco-Roman world. This is not to say that Christians necessarily confused the two, but rather that they chose an image of a pre-established deity with noble associations to portray their own idea of the sacred." (Yeomans)

Images of the sun god Helios, an earlier Titan who was identified with Apollo, appear in both Jewish synagogues and early Christian art. Helios in his son chariot depicted the sun as a ruling planet within the zodiac and the other signs of the zodiac were depicted within the sacred places of the Jews.

However there was already a trend in Hellenized Judaism throughout the Roman Empire to include pagan motifs and symbols within Jewish synagogues. Many Hebrew synagogues from the early centuries of the Common Era were found with mosaics of the signs of the zodiac, in particular representations of the Greek sun god Helios, who was identified with Apollo, as driving the chariot of the sun. In early Christian art, Christ was identified with the sun god, Helios.

"In a Christian funerary context, the image of Christ as Helios is commonly interpreted as being representative of the resurrection. In early Jewish depictions, it has been hypothesized that the image of Helios, or simply the sun as in the case of the mosaic at Sepphoris, represents God's omnipotence. In the context of ancient Jewish synagogues in Israel, the image of Helios is set within the context of zodiac symbols." (Yeomans)

Clement of Alexandria, an early Father of the Church, compared Christ to the pagan sun god who drove his sun chariot across the heavens. In his writings, Exhortation to the heathen, in which he tries to appeal to pagans to convert to Christianity, he likens Christ to that of Helios or Apollo by stating, "For the Sun of Righteousness, who drives his chariot over all, pervades equally all humanity." Clement combines the Biblical scriptures of Malachi by calling Christ, the Sun of Righteousness but also draws on the imagery of Apollo and Helios to create an image of Christ as the all-pervading solar deity who shines equally and promises salvation for all humans. (Murdoch)

Another figure associated with both Christ and Apollo was that of Orpheus. Orpheus was a son of Apollo and associated with his own mystery religion. Early Christianity also drew from sources such as mystery cults, which were often its rivals in popularity.

The mythological figure of Orpheus, who enchanted all of nature with his poetry and music, is another example of a pagan artistic type that was used in both early Christian as well as Jewish iconography. For the early Jews, the association of music and poetry with Orpheus likely led to the same image being used to represent King David, who famously sang his praises to God. Indeed, instances of David depicted with Orpheus imagery are well and firmly documented.

Equally well documented are images of Christ as Orpheus, particularly in the catacombs of Rome. One of the most famous aspects of the Orpheus myth from antiquity is the story of Orpheus's determined descent into Hades to rescue his love Eurydice, who had been snatched from him by an untimely death. While he was ultimately not successful in recovering Eurydice, he himself emerged from the underworld alive. This particular aspect of the myth resonated with early Christians, who saw this as an allegorical reference to Christ's descent into and return from the fiery depths of hell. Orpheus thus became a symbol of victory over death, and a symbol of eternal life. (Yeomans)

The two greatest feasts of the Christian year, Christmas and Easter are considered of paramount importance in the practice of Italian Catholic folk magic. It is believed that practitioners will initiate and teach the secrets of their Craft to family members on the vigils of these feasts.

The feast of Christmas, the nativity of Christ, is of course celebrated on the same day as the birthday of the Roman son god, Sol Invictus, the Unconquered Sun. Most likely this date was determined by the Church, as the Bible does not state when Christ was born, to defer pagan worship away from the solar deities and focus their attention on Christ. However it is also possible that the connection with Christ and solar divinities such as Apollo and Helios in the minds of the early Christians and Pagans also was an additional factor in determining the date of Christ's birth to be the same as that of the sun god.

The emperor Constantine, who officially ended the imperial persecution of Christianity and allowed the new religion to be tolerated was a devout worshipper of Sol Invictus. In the famous battle in which Constantine was the victor and assured his rise to the throne, he saw a cross of light within the sun and with it the words, with this you shall conquer.

Did Constantine, a devotee of Sol Invictus fighting for victory in the name of the pagan sun god or that of the newer divinity of Jesus? Was he acting out of faith or simply being pragmatic to the rise of Christianity?

We may never know what was going on in the mind of the emperor. He was only baptized as a Christian official as he lay close to dying. He continued to use the emblems of the sun and demanded that both Christians and pagans alike observe the day of the sun (our modern Sunday), as a day of rest, which was established by a previous emperor, Aurelius. It cannot be certain as to what his religious convictions truly were.

Italian witches are a pragmatic and practical sort. We see no issue in making use of both Catholic and pagan ritual and iconography in our craft. If the goddess Diana, is identified with the Virgin Mother of Christ and various female saints, why not Apollo with Jesus?

As a descendent of both pagan and Catholic ancestors, both traditions speak to my soul. When I feel the sun's warmth on my skin, I praise Apollo. When I attend the annual Easter Vigil to celebrate the resurrection of Christ, I feel the presence of my ancestors and sincerely rejoice as the lit candles fill the darkness of the church, announcing the resurrection of Jesus.

As an aside, a case can also be made for Christ being identified with Dionysus but that is a topic for another anthology.

I leave you with two pieces of sacred praise, one pagan and one Christian.

In the Christian hymn, Christ is referred to as the morning star, and in Italian witchcraft, the father of Aradia and brother of Diana is Lucifer, the morning star, who is most likely Apollo.

+++

First is the Orphic Hymn to Apollo (Thomas Taylor translation):

"Hear me entreating for the human kind,

Hear, and be present with benignant mind;

For thou survey'st this boundless æther all,

And ev'ry part of this terrestrial ball

Abundant, blessed; and thy piercing sight,

Extends beneath the gloomy, silent night;

Beyond the darkness, starry-ey'd, profound,

The stable roots, deep fix'd by thee are found."

+++

The Second is the Exultet or the Easter Proclamation of the Easter Vigil (an important feast in Italian stregoneria):

"Accept this Easter candle,

a flame divided but undimmed,

a pillar of fire that glows to the honor of God.

Let it mingle with the lights of heaven

and continue bravely burning

to dispel the darkness of this night!

May the Morning Star which never sets

find this flame still burning:

Christ, that Morning Star,

who came back from the dead,

and shed his peaceful light on all mankind,

your Son who lives and reigns for ever and ever. Amen."

+++

May the light of Christ and Apollo shine upon us all!

Works Cited

Murdoch, D.M.   Jesus as the Sun throughout History.

                  http://www.stellarhousepublishing.com/jesusasthesun.html

Yeomans, Sarah.   Borrowing from the Neighbors: Pagan Imagery in Christian Art.

                  http://www.biblicalarchaeology.org/daily/ancient-cultures/ancient-near-eastern-

                  world/borrowing-from-the-neighbors/

Rev. Dominick Guerriero has been a Tarot Card reader & Spiritual Advisor for 20+years. An initiate of Logunede in African-Brazilian Candomble, he draws also upon the stregoneria of his Italian heritage in his personal work. Dominick makes his home in the state of New York, USA.

Valedictory

Apollo, we lay these words into your hands, we entrust them to your ears and heart.

May all who have contributed to this weaving

find favor in your sight.

God of Light, may we be your Lights in this and every realm.

Esti ei nai!